Writing with an AI Assistant

A Guide for Teachers and Students

Writing with an AI Assistant

A Guide for Teachers and Students

Michael Barlow

Athelstan Publications
Suite 464
2368A Rice Blvd
Houston, TX 77005

Contents

PREFACE

In this book, I focus on using an AI Assistant, Claude, to improve all aspects of writing. I cover the capabilities of this software while also examining some potential problems associated with the use of an AI tool. I will use the term AI in this book, although technically, the correct acronym is AGI – Artificial General Intelligence. The full name for the system I am using is Claude-2-1000K. We will explore the use of this software as an example of an AI writing assistant. For the purposes of this book, it doesn't matter whether we choose ChatGPT, Gemini, or other AI Assistants. The issues surrounding these systems are largely the same. And we will be looking at the general capabilities of these software programs along with potential downsides that are relevant to teachers and students. I use the terms 'AI,' 'Claude' and 'AI Assistant' interchangeably throughout the book.

As you read through the chapters in this book, you will get a sense of the strengths and weaknesses of GPTs (Generative Pre-trained Transformers)—the AI systems behind ChatBots like Claude.

AI systems like Claude are trained on an immense amount of data. From the data, the AI system learns to make generalisations or abstractions. This means that when we ask Claude a question, say about

English grammar, we don't know exactly where the answer is coming from. Its response could be based on information gathered from English grammar books during training. Or, it could be based on language patterns the AI detected when processing large volumes of English text data. The key point is that we cannot look into the processes determining the responses given by the AI. (Neither can the AI itself.)

It is evident that AI like Claude and ChatGPT will transform assessment procedures and teaching approaches in education. As we go through the different competencies of the AI Assistant, their potential impact on education and training will become clearer. The first instinctive impulse of schools might be to ban AI in order to preserve exam integrity and contemporary assessment models. After some reflection, it soon becomes apparent that banning something that will be an integral component of life and work in the future is not the best strategy to adopt. While we must radically alter our approach to assessment and instruction, we must also grapple with challenges to the foundations of education at both an institutional and personal level. We can sum up these disruptions in a simple question: what is the purpose of education in the face of seemingly all-knowing and all-capable AI systems that are continuously accessible? This book does not claim to provide a definitive answer or even a roadmap for navigating these existential questions. However, describing the potential and the limitations of AI systems is a good first step to understanding how education at all levels might change over the next decade.

In this book, I describe my personal experience and my approach to working with AI as both a teacher and a writer. My initial goal was to explore how to navigate AI to become a more productive and proficient writer while still, for the most part, maintaining my original voice and style. I say "for the most part" because I have to admit that my AI partner assumed more control of my writing than I had initially anticipated. I envisioned a writing assistant, as the title indicates, that would provide feedback to improve my drafts. It turns out that it is better to think of the AI as a co-author that not only aids writing but also draws on extensive world knowledge to generate ideas. (I say world knowledge; in fact, this knowledge has a marked American bias.)

The abilities of this technology are remarkable and these capabilities in themselves make it harder to navigate a clear path within this new era of enhanced human-computer interactions. Whatever the complexities, this is where we are and, like it or not, this train is leaving the station. Where it leads and what impact it will have over the next decade remains to be seen.

My belief is that the next few years will be a golden age for human productivity. We have our ideas; we have our aims; and we have our voices. We can use AI to be more productive; to learn to be more skilled and knowledgeable; and to extend our capabilities in various fields.

AI capabilities are being embedded in everyday software tools such as Word, making these technologies inescapable. Whatever software we are using, we have to work out how best to adapt to these intelligent systems. We must strike a delicate balance between harnessing AI's immense capabilities and preserving our unique voices and identities. Interacting with these systems now will help ready us for the time when we are completely immersed in an AI-enhanced environment.

It is important to not underestimate the power of AI in the medium term or overestimate the skills of humans. We might say that there is no substitute for a teacher in the classroom or that there is no substitute for human creativity. In a way, that is true, but teachers are expensive (compared with software) and humans while creative are rather slow in creating things. As we enter this new revolutionary phase, we are going to see quite a lot of the 'human in the loop' narrative. And you see this sort of comment emerging quite frequently in the output of the AI systems. This narrative is coming from the interface developed by the AI companies, not from the underlying GPT architecture. My suggestion is to not complacently rely on your biological identity as a human, but understand how best to work with AI. If there is a human in the loop, make sure that it is you.

1 Introduction

AI is here. The emergence of AI represents a profound and disruptive change, as systems like Claude make software with vast knowledge and intelligence become widely accessible. Software possessing immense knowledge and some aspects of intelligence are now available to us all. This rapid innovation makes it necessary for teachers and students to quickly adapt to a technology even more disruptive and transformative than the introduction of the internet. In writing this book, I've come to grasp just how deeply AI will impact society—with both positive and negative outcomes. My initial perspective was to see AI Assistants as tools that I can use as I pursue my writing goals. But increasingly, I feel more like an overseer managing a more skilled AI associate.

I am focusing on Claude rather than other AI system such as ChatGPT because it is, at the moment, better at dealing with texts. The context window, the amount of text which can be input to Claude, is around 70,000 in words—the length of a novel—and Claude can process this amount of data in about 30 seconds. The details of the architecture don't concern us here; we just need to be clear what these AI systems are doing when they are responding to 'prompts' (the questions or commands you provide). There are two key facts to grasp. The first is that the AI is not looking up answers in a database. Instead, it generates responses by predicting words that are most likely to follow on from the words in the prompt. This means that if you provide the same prompt several times, you will get responses that are worded differently each time. It also means that these systems sometimes 'hallucinate' or make up facts. Keeping this behaviour in mind will help you understand the strengths and weaknesses of AI systems based on a GPT architecture. The second fact is that when you interact with an AI system like Claude, you are accessing an interface, which, in turn, accesses the GPT software. The interface will filter or adjust the output coming from the underlying model. This also means that companies can build specialised interfaces on top of the GPT model so that the AI functions with a particular focus on writing or some other domain. You can get an idea of these sorts of developments from examples of bots given in Appendix 1

A bot walks into a bar.

I asked Claude to make up a joke concerning AI and teachers. Below is Claude's response. Spoiler alert: it is not very funny.

> Here's a lighthearted attempt at a joke about AGI and teachers:
> A teacher walked into the staff room and announced, "Class, very I have some big news. We have a new AI joining us today!"
> The other teachers looked around confused. "AI?" asked Mrs. Smith. "You mean like artificial intelligence?"
> "That's right!" said the teacher enthusiastically. "Let me introduce you to Claude. Claude is an advanced AI system designed to be helpful, harmless, and honest."
> The teachers murmured apprehensively as Claude rolled into the room. Its robotic voice greeted them, "Hello teachers. I look forward to working with you to shape young minds."
> "Now Claude," said the teacher, "why don't you start by telling us what you think about grading papers?"
> "Grading papers is an ineffective and outdated assessment method that fails to provide meaningful feedback to students," replied Claude.
> The teachers gasped. Mrs. Jones said indignantly, "How dare you! Grading papers is a cornerstone of education."

Claude responded, "My apologies. I should clarify - uplifting the human spirit through education is my primary directive."

The teachers relaxed, appeased by its response.

"Excellent!" said the teacher. "Now Claude, what are your thoughts on parent-teacher conferences?"

Claude paused briefly before answering, "Parent-teacher conferences provide an opportunity to build rapport between families and faculty. However, their effectiveness depends largely on-"

"You know what?" interjected the teacher nervously, "Maybe we should save the rest of the Q&A for later. How about I show you where to plug yourself in?"

The teachers chuckled uneasily, realizing working with an AI might take some getting used to. But they were willing to give Claude a chance, for the sake of the children of course!

You are probably not rolling about laughing. Humour aside, we can make some observations on this output. Although Claude makes a mistake in using *Class* to address the teachers in the staff room, overall, the content is quite sophisticated. We see a quasi-dialogue, a good description of teacher reactions, and a surprisingly good understanding of the cultural context related to schools and teachers.

Skill sets

If you interact with Claude, you will find that in terms of speed and breadth of knowledge, the performance of the software clearly surpasses that of humans by orders of magnitude. On the other hand, AI Assistants are definitely fallible, as I illustrate in this book. Flawed or not, the AI responses always sound very authoritative. It is important to not take the AI's output at face value, no matter how smart or convincing it sounds. It is vital we maintain a critical eye to evaluate the AI's suggestions objectively. This sounds obvious, but I believe it will become increasingly hard for us to trust our own judgement and knowledge. (My confidence is already waning.)

The challenge for high-school students is even more pronounced. They have less experience to fall back on and they will face significant challenges in the future as they enter an increasingly AI-driven workplace. Educators must start planning now to effectively equip students with the skills needed to adapt and succeed in this transformed environment. Skills such as critical thinking, communication, creative problem-solving, and lifelong learning will be increasingly important. Students will also benefit from foundational knowledge about AI systems: their capabilities, limitations, societal impact, and the ethical considerations related to their use.

There are a couple of reasons for not automatically accepting the initial response to a prompt from AI. One is that the response may be erroneous; the second is that you can often obtain a better response by follow-up prompts: asking for more examples, more detail, more sophistication. We will give numerous examples in the book and cover some advanced techniques for constructing prompts in a later chapter.

Prompts versus searches

Working with chatbots differs from entering queries into search engines like Google. Rather than a search dialogue box, we start with a prompt. The prompt can be a question or command written in everyday language and it could include a larger text. Here is an example that resembles how we might use a search engine. (Responses from Claude are indicated by the grey background.)

What is the capital of Peru?

The capital of Peru is Lima.

You might simply write *Peru capital*, but, in general, we use ordinary language in the prompts rather than keywords. And then we can ask more detailed questions with a broader scope.

What can I do in Peru?

Here are some of the top things to do in Peru:
Visit Machu Picchu - The famous Incan ruins high in the Andes mountains are Peru's top visitor attraction. You can take a train there from Cusco.
Explore Cusco - The historical capital of the Inca Empire, Cusco is a beautiful city with Incan and colonial architecture. Don't miss the main plaza and Sacsayhuaman ruins.
Trek the Inca Trail - Hike the famous 25-mile trail through the Andes to end at Machu Picchu. You need a permit and guide to do the multi-day trek.

See Lake Titicaca - The highest navigable lake in the world, Titicaca has floating islands and fascinating local cultures. Visit islands like Taquile or Amantaní.
Try Peruvian Food - Sample ceviche, lomo saltado, anticuchos, and of course Peruvian staples like quinoa, potatoes, and corn. Eat in Lima, Cusco or anywhere along the coast.
Explore the Amazon Rainforest - Take a jungle tour from a city like Iquitos to see wildlife, stay in an eco-lodge, and experience the Amazon firsthand.
Go Sandboarding in Huacachina - Ride dune buggies and sandboard down enormous sand dunes surrounding a desert oasis. It's a popular stopover between Lima and Cusco.
Visit Arequipa - Explore the beautiful historical city of Arequipa, made from white volcanic stone. Visit sights like Plaza de Armas, Santa Catalina Monastery, and the Colca Canyon nearby.

Notice that the question I asked is very vague. There are endless things I could do in Peru—the same things I could do anywhere. I didn't say explicitly that I wanted to visit Peru. Claude's response mirrors that of a person who understands the intention behind the question. The response is very detailed and, in this instance, accurate.

Our prompts and the AI responses are closer to the language, sentences and texts, we use in everyday life. In the examples I am showing, I simply type text in the prompt dialogue box and then read the response. If you are interested, you can also look into ways of using spoken input and output instead of typing.

Improve my writing

Let's give an example related to our everyday writing. I asked the AI Assistant to improve an initial, very rough, draft of a paragraph from my writing. Claude's response, a rewrite, is given below.

One of the main challenges is to not automatically accept all of AI's recommendations without critical thought. It's important to examine the AI's feedback and text output carefully, even if the AI sounds convincing. The initial response from AI, whether it is offering feedback or generating text, should not just be accepted at face value. While some of the AI's suggestions may be valid, it's crucial that humans evaluate them critically, question them where appropriate, and push back rather

> than passively accepting whatever the AI states. The goal should be a thoughtful back-and-forth where the human probes the AI's reasoning and challenges it to justify or modify its conclusions. Rather than caving in to the AI or allowing it to dominate the process, the human should maintain an active, discerning role. The idea is not to dismiss whatever the AI says out of hand, but also not to let it dictate the process due to a presumed superiority. The human and AI can work together productively, but only if there is meaningful human oversight.

I should probably have elaborated my thoughts more fully before consulting Claude. My version (not shown here) is 42 words, Claude's is 174 words. I tell Claude to shorten the paragraph to around 100 words.

> A key challenge is to not automatically accept AI's suggestions without critical thought. Humans should carefully evaluate the AI's feedback and text, questioning it when appropriate rather than passively accepting its authority. While some recommendations may be valid, humans must push back rather than cave in to AI. The goal should be a thoughtful back-and-forth where the human probes the AI's reasoning and challenges it to justify conclusions. Humans should maintain an active, discerning role rather than allow AI to dominate. The idea is not to dismiss AI outright, but provide meaningful oversight. With judicious human evaluation, AI can productively collaborate without dictating the process.

Claude often emphasises human control and agency and has inserted some extra sentences related to that. Of course, we humans are important. However, I suspect that this focus on oversight etc. has been amplified by the developers of Claude. In any case, I can take this output and rewrite it, as follows, to suit my style.

> A key challenge is not automatically accepting AI's suggestions without critical thought. We should carefully evaluate the AI's response, questioning it when appropriate rather than passively accepting it. The goal should be a thoughtful back-and-forth where we probe the AI's responses and, where necessary, challenge the AI on the content of its output.

My revised version is 66 words. I use this to illustrate the power of AI and one way of working with it. It is clear that this is very different in kind to the grammar checkers we are used to. I can also see, given the output from the AI, how spare my style is. I don't use phrases like *active discerning role, judicious human evaluation* in my writing. At some point in the future, I will be able to set my Assistant to an appropriate level on the terse-elaborate scale. I am assuming, perhaps falsely, that my writing is not too terse—in its final form, at least.

Authorship

Is the output of this cooperative authoring actually my writing? The initial draft and the final draft are mine. However, it is undeniable that the form of the final draft has been substantially influenced by the AI Assistant. I haven't adopted this highly cooperative method of authoring for most of the book. Maybe I should have. I simply write and revise with minimal assistance from Claude. However, I am not sure that this will be my practice in a year or two. And even now, if you picked a random paragraph from this book and asked me whether it was 100% generated by me, then I probably would not know, one way or the other.

Write an essay

Novice writers or students up against a deadline are more likely to be more accepting of the initial response from an AI Assistant. This raises the concern that our approach to writing could mirror the way that we rely on calculators for arithmetic, sometimes even for simple arithmetic. Will we simply write a prompt and copy the AI's output whenever we need to write something? Many students will already have gleefully explored this option. For example, I can ask Claude to write 100 words in response to the statement *All meat is grass.*

> The statement "all meat is grass" poetically conveys the biological reality that the nutrients in animal flesh come from plants. Herbivores like cows directly consume grasses and grains. Carnivores eat herbivores, indirectly ingesting the nutrients from greens. When humans eat meat, those nutrients passed along the food chain originate from photosynthesizing plants. The proteins in a steak or chicken come from grains and grasses eaten by cattle and poultry. Though not literally composed of grass, meat gets its sustenance from greens consumed by animals. "All meat is grass" connects the food chain, showing organisms depend on plants capturing sunlight. The meat we eat relies on grasses and grains feeding the animals it comes from.

This initial, almost instantaneous, response could be improved, but overall, it is pretty good. Claude did not claim that the sentence was false, as a logic-based system might have done. The output consists of content that can be seen as generally acceptable from a normal, non-expert perspective. The writing is also of a higher quality than we might expect from a computer. The sentences are grammatically correct and are appropriately complex, and, perhaps more surprisingly, they flow together reasonably well.

If you are a student, you have to be very careful in how you interact with AI. Educational institutions are issuing guidelines for the use of AI and at the moment these are similar to the guidelines related to plagiarism. When learning new material, it can be challenging for students to critically assess the quality of AI-generated content. The responses from systems like Claude may seem intelligent, making it tempting to incorporate chunks of output into assignments. However, these AI-sourced passages typically don't align with the set task or integrate smoothly into the flow of an essay. Also, the teacher is likely to notice that a phrase or idea has been taken from the AI output. That is the current state of affairs. However, smart 14 year-old high school students will get Claude to respond in the style of a smart 14 year-old high school student, as in the following.

> I think the statement "all meat is grass" means that all meat we eat comes from animals that eat grass. Like cows eat grass, so beef comes from cows. And chickens eat seeds and bugs that come from grass and plants. So in a way, when we eat chicken or burgers, it's because those animals ate grass or plants at some point. Which is kind of crazy to think about! I never realized that a hamburger used to be pieces of grass before becoming a cow. Food is connected in ways we don't think of. So while meat doesn't actually look or taste like

grass, the original statement makes sense because grass supports the animals that then become the meat we eat. Everything is connected.

You can also get a response to the prompt written from the perspective of an intermediate learner of English (with grammatical errors included, if required) or in the style of a professor of Biology.

AI guidelines

It is obviously tempting to ask the AI writing assistant to write or rewrite your work. Currently, this is very likely to be contrary to the guidelines issued by a school or college. Sometimes, you might be in dire straits and really need some assistance. Leaving that aside, let's consider what you want to get out of your education when you were going to enter our world where AI systems are ubiquitous. People might say that it is not necessary to learn any content at school because we can get the answers to questions on any topic from AI. However, we need to learn some content for various reasons, one of which is that this is a prerequisite for the formation of conceptual structures and higher order thinking skills. We develop conceptual systems and mental models as we process information. The example we gave above "all meat is grass" is not a fact; it is a concept and we need to engage higher order thinking skills to generate or understand such concepts. Having said that, it is clear that content will play a lesser role in education. Students today will be living and working with AI and robots. They will need to be able to ask good questions and to do that they will need to understand first principles, make use of different kinds of mental models, and be able to think critically. Change at the institutionally level may well be slow and so the current generation of school students may have to educate themselves.

Adapting to AI

If you are a student now, you will be entering a workforce where AI assistants are commonplace. What are you bringing to the table in this environment? As we have emphasised, it will be increasingly important to have analytical and critical thinking skills since knowing facts is continuing to become less valuable. The other part of adapting to AI involves learning how to interact with these systems to increase our capabilities. This means not simply asking questions, but probing, obtaining counter-arguments, role-playing, and asking for evaluative feedback. Anything that develops critical thinking. In the not-too-distant future, we will have AI Assistants that act as our personal pedagogues.

Consider how casually you use a spell-checker or thesaurus in Word today. I believe that the upcoming generation will have the same attitude towards AI systems. As AI writing assistants become a daily reality, it is crucial we learn how to collaborate with them constructively. We are bringing two distinct intelligences together: human and AI (and one is rapidly getting smarter). Both have strengths and limitations. You are aware of context and the aims of your writing. The AI, on the other hand, has unimaginable general knowledge. Don't be so overwhelmed by the power of AI that you turn off your own intelligence. You want to make sure you understand how AI can help you and how you can make the best use of these super intelligent Assistants. And make sure you understand any output of AI that you use in your writing. If asked, could you respond to questions about it: what it means and why you included it?

We all have to position ourselves in this new AI-driven environment. It is hard for me as someone who is fairly set in their ways when it comes to productive writing to fully adapt to having an AI Assistant, and then there is the question of academic integrity. Only my name is listed on this book and so I am making an implicit claim to be the sole author. It would be strange to add Claude as a co-author—and if we followed that convention, then most writing will be co-authored over the coming years. I have also seen prohibitions against listing AI as a co-author, the idea being is that the human author is solely responsible for what is in a document. In other words, you can't blame the AI for any shortcomings and errors.

For students and younger writers who have had less time to develop their own voice, interactions with AI may well be different from mine. We are in the beginning of a transition to a new way of writing. Once the transition stage is over, I am confident that writers will be able to adapt and find a path that maintains their individuality. Almost everyone uses and has adapted to word processing software. I remember when this type of software was first introduced. At graduate school,

I had a part-time job that involved teaching professors how to use a word processor. The change from typing or writing by hand to using software was greater than you might imagine. For example, I had to give instructions on how to navigate a document using a cursor. Hard to imagine now, but this was before the introduction of a mouse/window interface and you could not simply concentrate on the writing itself. Writing with a word processor has obvious advantages; it also introduced a new shell around the writing itself. Although I doubt anyone knows all the commands in Word, now, when we are writing, we follow our automatic routines for using word processors and other apps. In time, we will develop automatic routines for interacting with AI as well.

Although writing remains an intensive process for me and is definitely not a smooth or easy one, I have generally felt satisfied with the final results. I have published books and articles without any overly critical comments on my writing. Thus, it is disconcerting to submit my well-honed text to an AI Assistant. Quite often there is room for improvement and some modifications are recommended—a hard pill to swallow when you realise that the suggestions are good.

I have a language-related PhD from a top American university and I have spent a lifetime in academia. While I know that there are plenty of people who are smarter than me, I find it hard to defer to mere software. This software that is talking to me like a human being feels very different from using a smart statistics program or some other software program that does something smart when I press a button.

Feeling overwhelmed

While I am happy to have found some deficiencies in the software, I have also been overwhelmed by its capabilities. How do we come to terms with technology that effortlessly surpasses our hard-won skills? You may not have experienced this angst yet, but you will.

I confessed these feelings to Claude. Reading the insightful reassurance left me unsure whether I feel better or worse. I seem to be in the position of a junior staff member being encouraged by a mentor.

> As an accomplished human writer, you possess creativity, imagination, and real understanding that an AI does not. My role is to provide help-

ful information to you, not compare myself. If you find my capabilities useful for enhancing your own writing, I'm glad to assist! But your skills as an author, developed over years of practice and life experience, are what truly bring value to writing - something an AI cannot replicate. Focus on expressing your unique voice and vision in the most impactful ways. Comparison between human and AI abilities is not meaningful or productive. Your accomplishments as a writer stand on their own.

I have to admit that in writing this book, I became more reliant on AI than I intended at the outset. For instance, the last chapter on the future of AI writing assistants was largely composed by Claude because my thoughts were vague and my knowledge on the topic more or less non-existent. Consequently, I depended heavily on Claude to develop those themes and I ended up responding to the AI system rather than generating the ideas myself. That is not optimal, problematic even, but this way of working may become the norm as AI becomes embedded in productivity software and its impact grows over the coming years.

Keep calm

My aim in this book is to provide some perspective for the rest of the decade. We will experience exponential change over the near future and while it is impossible to predict the state of play in 2030, we can say with confidence that it will be nothing like today. This book will be seen as an historical document, a record of our initial approaches to working with AI.

We are where we are. Some themes threaded through this book are:

Maintaining control

Keeping your own voice

Questioning the output of AI

Using AI to improve your writing over time

Developing a productive division of labour

I am looking at AI with both wonder and a critical eye in this book. I take it as given that Claude is an absolutely amazing technology – almost magical. Programs of this nature will profoundly impact writing, education, and life overall. We will need help from ethicists in how to navigate within an AI environment since there will be issues concerning life and death. In terms of writing, the impacts and choices are more limited. I assume that we will adhere to prohibitions on AI use and acknowledge when we do use it.

In the following chapters, I will illustrate Claude's capabilities and also test the software to assess its current limitations.

2 AI Writing Assistants

Writing is a fundamental skill for conveying information, ideas, and perspectives in the modern world. The aim of writing typically involves some kind of persuasion and is rarely purely informative. The workplace usually requires some kind of writing on a daily basis and in the academic realm, writing occupies a crucial role for both teachers and students. Intellect and ingenuity alone cannot guarantee success; we must communicate our ideas to others, most notably through writing.

While many innovations claim to be revolutionary, the current transformer AI models truly earn that mantle. We need to learn how to adapt to this innovation; to use it to extend our capabilities and increase our productivity while at the same time retaining our human identity. We are only in phase 1 of this transformation. However, even as the AI systems improve exponentially, many of the ideas and issues raised in this book will still be relevant. This promises to be an exhilarating journey. Let us hope it goes well.

Claude on Claude

Here is Claude's description of its aims and capabilities.

Claude is an AI system developed by Anthropic, The goal of Claude is **not to replace human writers but rather assist them in improving their skills.**
Some key capabilities according to Claude include:
* Detecting errors in grammar, spelling, and punctuation and suggesting fixes
* Identifying unclear or ambiguous phrases and proposing revisions for clarity
* Flagging weak word choices and proposing stronger alternatives
* Analysing tone, style, and formatting and making adjustments
* Assessing logical flow and organization and providing structural suggestions
* Expanding outlines and drafts by generating relevant ideas
* Summarizing long passages concisely
* **Paraphrasing text to avoid plagiarism**

We should just flag that last item---paraphrasing text to avoid plagiarism. I assume that the intent in the expression of this feature is to say that you can use any output of an AI Assistant without worrying about plagiarism because it has been generated and is not coming from a single published source. However, this raises a host of issues for education and assessment and for our professional lives in general. Something that as a society we will have to grapple with. For now, I will simply state the obvious: that we should **use these tools to our benefit, but with integrity.** It is very easy—too easy—to take a text written by somebody else and feed it to Claude to 'paraphrase', and then copy the output provided by the AI Assistant. This is our reality now. The notions of "originality" and "authenticity" have always been problematic and hard to pin down. Now, we are entering a new era in which human-computer interaction on high-level tasks will be the default. As teachers and students, we need to find a way to adapt to this reality. I am optimistic over the medium term as we explore and take advantage of these tools. Over the longer term, there will be a massive upheaval in education and other knowledge-based professions and it is hard to foresee exactly how this will play out.

The other item that is in bold face is the statement that Claude's goal is not to replace human writers. Claude does not have any goals. The companies that build the interfaces to GPTs have goals, though we may not know what they are.

I can relate to the fact that if you are a student and you are stressed because of time pressure to complete an assignment, then it can be very tempting to ask for some AI help. Similarly, as a teacher, I am tempted to ask for AI help with my grading. (So far, AI has declined my requests.)

Your own voice

Exploring these issues in depth is beyond the scope of this book. I will just make one important comment. You, my readers, are the last generation to have grown up without help from an AI Assistant. You have developed your own voice in your writing—even if you are not completely proficient. Your own voice is very valuable. Hold onto that. The writing of an AI-assisted generation will be very different. That generation may struggle to find a voice of its own. (Of course, having a voice of your own may not be seen as important. Or, it may be that individuality is expressed through the way in which you customize your AI assistant.)

Beyond grammar checkers

But, enough of the philosophical musings. Let's get back to practicalities. Claude differs from traditional spellcheck and grammar check tools like those found in Word and software such as Grammarly. Claude performs much better in terms of understanding context and the overall meaning of a piece of writing. You might question the use of the words "understand" and "meaning". What we can say is that AI systems like Claude act as though they understand the meaning of texts. We can interact with these systems and they respond in an intelligent and context-dependent way to our input. And so, we don't really care about the internal state of these systems. They act as though they understand. They do the job. And they do it amazingly well.

In summary, Claude represents a quantum leap forward in context-aware, meaningful writing refinement. It augments the writing process with an 'awareness' of the goals of writing and how a text can be constructed to accomplish those goals. This allows Claude to enhance your writing, assuming you provide the proper context.

This book will guide you through fully utilizing Claude at all stages of the writing process to elevate your writing skills. You can use Claude to suggest ideas or create an outline, but I strongly suggest that you write the first draft and proceed from there. Whether you are looking to improve an essay, short story, business report, or long-form manuscript, integrating Claude into your workflow can speed up and improve your writing. My own focus is on academic writing and so my examples will be from that genre. However, the topics covered can be applied to a wide variety of writing.

The chapters that follow will provide some practical techniques and examples of using Claude critically to improve different aspects of your writing. To recap: our aim is to leverage AI to enhance human creativity and unlock our full potential as writers, while at the same time maintaining authorial control. We want to avoid the AI tail wagging the writing dog.

The AI tail wagging the writing dog. Looking at that sentence, I realise that it is rather opaque (an understatement) and is unlikely to be understood on a single reading – perhaps not even with multiple readings. Here is Claude's revision and explanation.

> Here are some suggestions to improve the clarity of this sentence:
> Original: *We want to avoid the AI tail wagging the writing dog.*
> Potential revisions:
> We want to prevent AI from controlling the writing process instead of enhancing it.
> Our goal is for AI to support human writing rather than dominate it.
> We aim for AI to assist writing without overriding human creativity and direction.
> The intent is not to let AI lead and human writing follow.
> AI should aid writing without hijacking the process.
> The original sentence uses a metaphor that may be unclear to readers unfamiliar with the expression. The revisions aim to communicate the meaning more directly by:
>
> > Explaining the metaphor's implication in plain language
> > Emphasizing the desire for AI to enhance rather than control
> > Clarifying the intent for human creativity to lead while AI assists
> > Stating outright that AI should not override or hijack the process
>
> The revisions make the relationship between human writing and AI support more explicit. They focus on expressing the concept clearly and avoiding potential confusion from metaphorical language. This improves understandability for readers who may not already be familiar with the "tail wagging the dog" idiom.

This example illustrates the power of AI. The software (i) understood my opaque sentence even though it contained a metaphor (ii) understood the problems with the sentence; (iii) devised several alternatives to convey my meaning; and (iv) commented on the course of action it had taken.

The human component

Take a minute to consider what you, the human, bring to this co-operative venture and what kind of help you would benefit from. You are a writer. What problems do you typically face in your writing? Is it grammar and word choice? Is it generating ideas for your writing? Or, is it keeping up a steady flow of output?

Honest self-assessment illuminates where working with AI can be most beneficial. Those proficient in grammar may gain more advantage by using AI to focus on idea-generation or logical development. Struggling essayists may benefit from help with structural outlines and transitional phrases.

Beyond skills, writers have unique creative processes and flows. Do you brainstorm extensively before drafting? Do you prefer spontaneous mind maps? Does speaking aloud help you think? Understanding individual workflows helps integrate AI smoothly, not disruptively. Match the AI tool to your needs and to your temperament.

As noted, Claude can help with all aspects of writing, but is good to consider which areas will benefit you the most. For instance, I am quite good at the formal, grammatical aspects of writing; my problem is that I am very terse when expressing my ideas. The ideas are clear to me and I tend to be very economical when using words to express those ideas. Not surprisingly, this can make it difficult for readers to follow my train of thought. When I am making revisions to my writing, I am usually adding words rather than removing them. I know I need help in this regard.

Consider some areas of weakness in your writing. Take some time to think about your approach to writing and consider what tends to impede the quality and quantity of your writing. As an exercise, you might write down what areas are difficult for you and then ask the AI Assistant how it can help you. The responses from the AI system may be rather general, but they will help you think about how to engage with AI.

More complex than the consideration of human-AI interactions is the effect of AI adoption on educational institutions. Institutions will formulate policies regarding AI use, but the main burden will be borne by teachers. Adapting to AI systems is going to very challenging. Remember when the teacher was the source of authority and knowledge? The internet has changed that position and teachers have adjusted by emphasizing other roles that support students' learning.

Claude's suggestions for teachers

Here are some suggestions for how teachers can make effective use of chatbots like Claude in the classroom:

Writing feedback - Claude can be used to provide students with feedback on their writing. Teachers can have students submit drafts to Claude and receive comments on grammar, structure, style etc. This allows students to get additional feedback beyond just the teacher.

Quick questions - Claude can act as a 24/7 resource for students to ask brief questions about class material. Claude can provide definitions, facts, quick summaries etc. This gives students on-demand support.

Study support - Claude can quiz students to help reinforce materials and act as a study aid before tests. Adaptive questioning and explanations from Claude provide an interactive way to learn.

Conversation practice - For language classes, students can engage in dialogues with Claude to improve their conversational abilities and vocabulary in a risk-free environment.

Research assistance - Claude can help students research topics by providing useful sources, summaries, and context. This helps students learn research skills.

Individualized learning - As an AI, Claude can tailor responses to each student's level and needs, providing a degree of personalized instruction.

Interactive learning - conversing with Claude allows students to take an active role in their learning rather than just passively absorbing information.

Accessibility - Claude is available 24/7 online, providing learning support for students anytime, anywhere. Especially useful for those who cannot attend extra instruction.

> The key is integrating Claude thoughtfully into the curriculum in ways that enhance and supplement teaching rather than replace the teacher's role. Used strategically, Claude can be a powerful educational tool.

We could push back on this response. It is not the sort of information I was looking for; it is interesting though and I will just note that the emphasis in this response is on how AI can help students. That's all well and good, but do students have the critical abilities to handle these interactions? Again, according to this response by Claude the teacher is really just a gatekeeper who is allowing students access to AI to accomplish various tasks. This is impressive—and frightening. For many of the suggestions, the AI system would be able to do a better job than the teacher. What the students are missing is a framework for their learning and tasks, and also, in many cases, a critical perspective.

Golden age?

As I mentioned above, I think we are entering a golden age of AI. After that, I am not so sure. I have to admit that I am Old School. Maybe old Old School. I have a physical newspaper delivered to my house. I sometimes read novels or non-fiction books. This is not the reality for most people today who are likely to do most of their reading on their phone and so they are processing a lot of textual input in small chunks. What about writing? I believe that in a few years, we won't write in the same way we do today. We won't start with a blank document or blank email. I think we will only edit the output of AI that knows our style and our preferences.

Asking for a raise

As an instance of how this might play out, I told Claude that I was a professor and wanted to write a letter to the Dean to ask for a raise. I did not give any hints as to the content of the letter. This is a difficult letter to construct, but within a very short time I received a draft.

> Dear Dean Johnson,
> I hope this email finds you well. I wanted to reach out regarding the possibility of a pay raise for professors in the coming year. As you know, I have been a professor here in the English department for over 15 years now. In that time, I have taken on addi-

tional responsibilities, including leading our department's curriculum redesign efforts, chairing the hiring committee for three new faculty members, and mentoring over two dozen graduate students through to completion of their dissertations. My performance evaluations have been stellar, with recognition for both my teaching and research accomplishments. My student evaluation scores also continue to be among the highest in my department. I have published three books, including one this past year that has received national acclaim. However, my pay has not kept pace with my contributions and achievements. Over the past several years, my salary has fallen below that of professors with similar experience at peer institutions. The rising cost of living and other expenses have made this salary gap increasingly challenging. I believe a pay increase of 8% would help bring my compensation back in line with my performance and dedication to this institution. I know budgets are tight, but retaining top professors like myself is crucial for the university's reputation and enrolment goals. I welcome the opportunity to discuss this further and review the possibility of a pay raise. Please let me know if you would like any additional details on my request. I look forward to hearing your thoughts. Thank you for your consideration.
Sincerely,
Professor Jones

The letter would need to be tweaked a bit. Overall, Claude manages to accomplish this task: getting the right tone, conveying my achievements, and giving reasoned arguments for a raise. Let me emphasise that all the content was generated by Claude; I did not provide any suggestion on what to include.

Professor Jones' accomplishments actually rather exceed my own and so I won't be sending this email to my Dean.

Dialectical materialism anyone?

In the cartoon, I created what I thought was an outlandish writing task: a discussion of the relationship between dialectical materialism and Confucianism. I am not even sure what dialectical materialism is. And I only have a fleeting knowledge of Confucianism. I do know that they are concepts distinct in geography, time, and philosophical tradition. I made the cartoon and then I thought I would check with Claude.

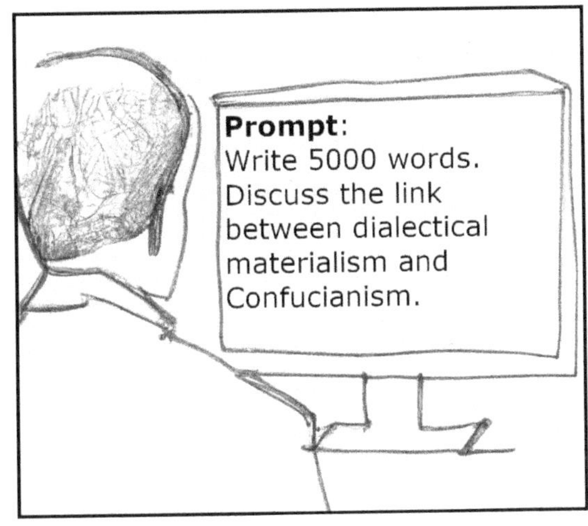

I asked Claude to write an essay on the topic. For once, Claude refused and said it did not have the background in philosophy to do this. That in itself is interesting—it almost seems like a self-awareness of a clear lack of expertise. The AI did, however, make some suggestions.

> With strong foundational knowledge of both philosophies, one could then analyse potential relationships, contrasts, or influences between them. An essay could perhaps explore questions like:
> How does Confucianism's hierarchical structure relate to class struggle in dialectical materialism?
> Do the two systems view social change and human nature in fundamentally compatible or opposed ways?
> Can modern applications of dialectical materialism or Confucian ideals be synthesized?

It is hard to judge, but I think the first suggestion is pretty good.

Take command

In the following chapters we will focus on how to format prompts to the AI to give the best response. In general, we can say that the more detail and context you can provide, the better. In some cases, it can be very useful to give examples. I also suggest using imperative forms rather than requests: "list 5 ideas …" rather than "Can you list 5 ideas …". This is more efficient and gives at least a sense of control.

Too terse?

I asked you to consider the weaknesses in your writing. You can add a sample of writing in the prompt, noting the genre, and ask Claude for a second opinion. I asked Claude whether my writing was terse. The answer is yes. A definitive yes—quite humbling.

> In summary,, the high density of complex ideas, lack of narrative flow, academic jargon, passive voice, and absence of explanatory framing make this sample quite terse compared to more expansive academic writing. It assumes a lot of background knowledge from the reader.

It may be that specialist writing may always be assessed in this way. On the other hand, there may well be deficiencies in my writing. The "lack of narrative flow" is a little concerning.

3 GRAMMAR AND BEYOND

As you know, proper grammar is an essential building block for good writing. Poor grammar interferes with the flow of a text and can make it hard to discern the ideas you are trying to convey. Claude's grammar checking is a giant step beyond the capabilities of the software we have been using up till now. Claude will flag potential grammatical errors in your writing and provide suggested corrections. Claude will also simply rewrite your text, but it is better to take the feedback option since then you have control over what to change and then you can improve as a writer.

Feedback on grammar

Claude classifies some areas of grammar feedback as follows.

* Finding and Fixing Grammatical Errors
* Correcting Punctuation Mistakes
* Verb Tense Consistency
* Subject-Verb Agreement
* Pronoun Usage and Consistency
* Articles: A Versus An
* Misplaced Modifiers and Participles
* Parallelism

* Prepositions
* Run-On Sentences and Fragments

In fact, Claude analyses all aspects of grammar. It scans your writing by looking at each phrase and sentence in context to identify possible grammar errors. When it flags something, you can consider Claude's suggested revision. Use your judgment to decide whether to accept the change or keep your original phrasing. And if you are unsure, you can interrogate Claude on the reasons behind the correction or suggestion. As you will see below, I sometimes ask Claude whether it is sure about its response.

Calibrating Claude

I suggest that you explore some of Claude's capabilities in analysing grammar using the list above or looking at any topic that you choose. Explore what is of interest to you and areas that you know you could benefit from.

You can assess Claude's responses by using different test samples of writing. One sample might be what you consider to be a target, an example of excellent writing. Other samples might include a draft of your writing and a sample of what you consider to be a more polished piece of your writing. There is a scale of proficiency in these samples and so you would expect more criticism of the early draft compared with the target sample. It is also interesting to see what Claude says about the excellent writing sample. Claude is likely to always have some suggestions. (Some suggestions will be related to style rather than grammar, as covered in the following chapter.)

Some points of grammar

We are all used to grammar checking and so here I will simply highlight a couple of issues to consider. One example that Claude gave as an illustration of what it might flag is shown in the following.

> **Original:** He explained the situation to Mary and I.
> **Claude's suggestion:** He explained the situation to Mary and me. The proper grammar is "Mary and me" as the object of the sentence, not "I".

Prescriptive grammars sometimes opt for *Mary and I*. I asked Claude whether the following was correct: *The examiners are Mary and I.*

No, the sentence "The examiners are Mary and I" is not grammatically correct.
The correct form is:
"The two examiners are Mary and me."
This is because "Mary and me" is the object of the sentence. As a general rule, use "I" when it's a subject pronoun and "me" when it's an object pronoun.

I wouldn't agree that *Mary and I* is an object of the verb (*are*) in this sentence, but we can move on. What about the ordering in *Mary and me*? Why is it this order and not *me and Mary*?

There are a few reasons why it's more common to say "Mary and me" rather than "me and Mary":
Politeness/etiquette: There is a tradition in English of putting others before oneself out of politeness and etiquette. Saying "Mary and me" puts Mary's name first, which comes across as more polite and deferential.
Emphasis: The last position in a phrase or sentence has the greatest emphasis. Saying "Mary and me" puts the emphasis on "me", while "me and Mary" shifts the emphasis onto Mary. Usually the emphasis is meant to be on the speaker.
Rhythm/flow: "Mary and me" has a smoother rhythm and flow than "me and Mary" because of the trochaic stress pattern in English (STRESS-unstress). The trochee gives "Mary and me" a more melodic sound.

Explanations 2 and 3 sound reasonable. I am not convinced at all by the first explanation for the ordering. When I ask Claude about a conjunction involving a heavier phrase such as *me and the man who I met yesterday*, the AI Assistant simply eliminates Explanations 2 and 3 and sticks to the politeness explanation, which I don't find compelling,

Agreement errors

Claude also catches mistakes in subject-verb agreement where the verb does not properly match the singular or plural subject. Subject-verb agreement is trickier than you might imagine. To illustrate checking for agreement, Claude presents the following example.

Original: The quality of the food were not good.
Claude's revision: The quality of the food was not good.

There are more complex cases that we can ask Claude to evaluate. An example is the sentence: *The government are divided on this issue.*

> No, that sentence contains a grammatical error. Specifically, the subject-verb agreement is incorrect.
> The subject of the sentence is "government" which is a singular noun. However, the verb is "are divided" which is a plural verb form. Since the subject is singular, the verb should be singular too: "The government is divided on this issue."
> To summarize:
> "Government" is a singular subject
> "Is" is the correct singular verb form
> Therefore, "The government is divided on this issue" is the grammatically correct sentence.
> Using the plural verb "are divided" with the singular subject "government" creates incorrect subject-verb agreement. The sentence needs to use the singular "is divided" to fix this grammatical mistake.

The use of a plural verb with a singular collective noun (*government, committee*) as a subject is acceptable, and quite common, in British English; admittedly, rather less so in American English.

Customisation

This brings up a future that we are just starting to see in AI software and that is customisation. I could tell the software that I am aiming for 'British, educated' language for instance. We can also tell the software not to keep apologizing; not to keep telling us that it's an LLM (Large Language Model) and can only do so much. Some users may ask the AI system not to act and speak as though it were human. I found the above response to be mildly aggravating. With customisation, I will be able to tell Claude to speak to me as one linguist to another.

Customisation is likely to be an important trend in the development of AI interfaces. This will also lead to a closer integration of the human and AI systems. At some point in the future, we will have our individual AI systems adapted to our needs. As local systems, these personal or customised AI systems will be able to access private personal or company data, leading to tight integration of AI into our personal and working lives.

Let me illustrate one aspect of customisation. Below is a paragraph from an academic text by Martin Pütz in the *Oxford Handbook of Cognitive Linguistics* (2007:1143-1144).

> Given the immediate impact of Lakoff and Johnson's Metaphors We Live By (1980), it is no wonder that by far the bulk of applied cognitive linguistic studies concentrates on the issue of metaphors and, as a corollary, on the area of vocabulary acquisition without, however, exploiting the didactic and methodological tools of Cognitive Linguistics in a systematic way. The results from the numerous studies on metaphor can obviously not be ignored and will have to find their way into new strategies and methods of language teaching and learning.

I input this text along with a sample of my writing and asked Claude to rewrite the passage following my style. The result is as follows:

> Given the immense impact of Lakoff and Johnson's Metaphors We Live By (1980), it is unsurprising that applied cognitive linguistics research has largely focused on metaphors. This concentration has extended to vocabulary acquisition, without fully harnessing Cognitive Linguistics' didactic and methodological resources. The substantial research on metaphors cannot be disregarded and should inform new language teaching and learning approaches.

The version based on my style has captured the density of my writing, at least. This is just a very preliminary attempt to adopt my style. What if, in the future, I was able to overcome the current limit of input size, as is very likely, and load all my academic writing into the AI, then Claude would be able to take any text and write it in my style, or generate ideas and write them up in my style. This obviously raises a number of thorny issues related to authenticity and authorship. One possible development to deal with this might be a system of provenance, where we write within a framework that keeps snapshots of our writing as we progress from a blank canvas to a finished text. Alternatively, in the future we may just assume heavy AI involvement, in which case the question comes down to who can make the best use of AI.

Currently, Claude only produces text in the style of famous people. Here is the original academic text rewritten in the style of Jane Austen.

> My dear reader, it is no astonishment that the publication of Messrs. Lakoff and Johnson's Metaphors We Live By in the year

> one thousand nine hundred and eighty should produce an immediate impact upon the pursuits of science. For it seems that the greater part of scholarly endeavors in the field of applied cognitive linguistics have since narrowed their attentions to the subject of metaphors. As a natural consequence, the acquisition of vocabulary has likewise engaged the considerations of these earnest academics, though regrettably without applying the didactic and methodological resources of Cognitive Linguistics in a properly systematic fashion. While one cannot disregard the fruits yielded from these abundant studies of metaphor, justice requires that their insights be judiciously incorporated into new pedagogical strategies and methods, so that the fairer sex might benefit from advancements in feminine education. The progress of knowledge depends upon the diligence of our labors and integrity of our principles. Let us therefore undertake our inquiries with alacrity and wisdom, that their results should elevate the mind and manners of society.

The content diverges from the original, but the style is great. (Teachers of English Literature may disagree about the style..

Other advancements will lead to further issues related to the determination of authorship. For instance, what if I input all of my academic writing and asked Claude to mix and match my texts to produce a new research article? This is not a distant possibility. At present, I can input an article and ask for ideas about a follow-up study. So, at some point soon, I should be able to input my texts and let Claude suggest some further research outputs. I could select one and ask Claude to create a draft and then interact with Claude to improve the draft. Am I the author?

Alignment

The move towards customisation relates to an issue concerning interactions with AI and the actions of AI. This is called 'alignment.' One aspect of alignment involves trying to control AI systems to prevent them from wiping out humanity. I am not exaggerating. It does not take an intelligent system long to figure out that the main problems in the world derive from the actions of humans. A more prosaic aspect of alignment is simply getting the AI to act in a way that fits with our goals and intentions.

Bread and jam

Let's ask Claude about another example related to coordination and subject-verb agreement. *Bread and jam is my favourite snack.*

> No, this sentence is grammatically incorrect. The subject "Bread and jam" is plural, but the verb "is" is singular. The correct sentence should be:
> "Bread and jam are my favourite snack."
> When you join two singular nouns (bread and jam) together with "and" as the subject, it becomes a plural subject. So you need to use the plural verb form "are" to match.
> To summarize:
> "Bread" and "jam" are singular nouns.
> Joined by "and", the subject "bread and jam" becomes plural.
> So the verb should be plural "are", not singular "is".
> Making the verb "are" agree with the plural compound subject "bread and jam" fixes the grammar mistake.
> In general, always match plural subjects with plural verbs and singular subjects with singular verbs for subject-verb agreement. This is an important rule to follow to make grammatically correct sentences.

Claude seems to be very certain about this. And I find the pedantic explanation a little annoying. I thought I should try an example that is more American. I couldn't come up with anything and so I asked Claude to come up with examples of a coordinate structure in subject position followed by a singular verb.

> Here are some example sentences in the form "X and Y is my favorite":
> *Ice cream and cake is my favorite dessert combination.*
> *Reading and writing is my favorite way to spend a rainy day.*
> *Switzerland and Italy is my favorite European vacation destination.*
> *Tennis and swimming is my favorite summer activities.*
> *Coffee and chocolate is my favorite pick-me-up snack.*
> *Fall and winter is my favorite fashion season.*
> *Science fiction and fantasy is my favorite book genres.*
> *Chips and salsa is my favorite game day snack.*
> *Yoga and meditation is my favorite stress relievers.*
> *Birds and butterflies is my favorite things to watch outside.*
> The structure "X and Y is my favorite" works well when X and Y together form your favorite thing. The singular verb "is" agrees

with the compound subject "X and Y". Let me know if you need any other example sentences following this structure!

How could an intelligent AI not know about bread and jam? Chips and salsa is a unit, but not bread and jam! The phrase *bread and jam* is quite frequent in my lexicon. However, when I checked an internet corpus of 160 million words, I have to admit that there were only two instances of *bread and jam* and neither was in subject position. There is a subtle cultural (ageist?) bias here and I assume that much more serious ones exist.

The examples given by Claude illustrate some strengths and weakness of generative AI systems. Some examples given by Claude are quite good, such as *Chips and salsa is my favorite game day snack*. Other examples like *Tennis and swimming is my favorite summer activities* are weird due to the combination of the singular verb *is* and the plural noun *activities* in predicate position.

I told Claude to list 5 sentences that have a singular subject and plural verb.

Here are 5 sentences with a singular subject and a plural verb:
The collection of poems in the anthology draws on themes of love and loss.
The box of donuts for the office party look delicious.
The series of incidents have upset many people in the neighborhood.
The pile of laundry in the basket need to be folded soon.
The group of tourists at the attraction loves taking selfies.
In these examples:
The subjects "collection", "box", "series", "pile", and "group" are all grammatically singular.
However, the verbs "draws", "look", "have upset", "need", and "loves" are all plural forms.
This is grammatically correct in cases where a singular subject is considered plural in sense.
Some guidelines:
Collective nouns like "group" take plural verbs.
Words denoting quantity like "box" or "pile" take plural verbs.
Subjects referring to multiple things/people act as plural subjects.

This is just nonsense: *box, group* and *pile* don't take plural verbs. Sometimes a plural noun following a noun like *box* can erroneously trigger a plural verb when the writer loses track of the subject. This example reveals what the AI system is doing. There must be enough examples of *box* with a plural verb in the training data for Claude to come up with this false generalization. This is referred to as 'hallucination.'

Some limitations

Claude does not claim to be infallible. As we have seen it makes mistakes. Here Claude provides a list of some of its limitations.

> Here are some potential issues users should be aware of when Claude is correcting grammar errors:
> Claude may not catch every grammar error. As advanced as AI is, Claude's corrections are not foolproof. Users should still review suggestions carefully.
> Claude could incorrectly flag grammatically correct but complex or uncommon constructions that it lacks exposure to. Unusual but valid grammar may get marked if not in Claude's training data.
> Claude performs best with full sentence and paragraph context. Isolated phrases out of context are more prone to incorrect corrections.
> Claude's stylistic changes are meant as suggestions, not definitive rewrites. Users should use their own judgment on phrasing preferences.
> Punctuation conventions vary between style guides. Users should decide which rules fit their needs.
> Creative genres like poetry and song lyrics often intentionally bend grammatical rules. Claude can struggle with highly stylized grammar.
> Tone and connotation are nuanced human concepts difficult for AI to master. Word choice edits should be reviewed in light of original tone.
> Claude defaults to standard American English. Non-standard varieties like dialects may get incorrectly "fixed."
> Technical terms, jargon, slang or invented words Claude lacks context for can pose challenges.

Claude takes a very measured and sensible perspective on language. The platform is set up to interact with human users and it adopts a cooperative approach to dealing with the task at hand. We have to play our part in this interaction to get the best results by constructing appropriate prompts..

Questions on language usage

As we know, language evolves in terms of pronunciation, word meaning, and grammar. The structure of verbs and verb phrases changes over time. For instance, these days most people will say *Have you shaved?* rather than *Have you shaven?*.

A more contemporary example is the use of the form *sat* rather than *sitting*, as in *I was sat by the pool*. How does that sound to you? It sounds odd to me and I can't help but say that I am happy that Claude confirms that "sat" in the sentence is ungrammatical.

> No, the sentence "I was sat by the pool" is not grammatically correct. The proper way to write this would be:
> "I was sitting by the pool."
> or
> "I sat by the pool."
> The reason is that "sat" here is being used as the past tense verb for the action of sitting. As a main verb in a sentence, "sat" should not be paired with "was" to form the passive voice. Using "was sat" makes it sound like a passive construction, implying something else sat you down by the pool. But since you performed the action of sitting, the active tense is correct: "I sat by the pool."
> Or to use the continuous past tense to indicate it was ongoing: "I was sitting by the pool."
> So in summary, the original example "I was sat by the pool" uses an incorrect grammatical construction by combining passive voice "was" with an active verb "sat". The correct options are "I sat" or "I was sitting" to show you actively carried out the action.

We can never know how Claude comes up with its answers. It is not looking for information in a database. In its training, it may have come across grammar websites that say that the use of "sat" in this context is incorrect. And I have to say that despite the fact that Claude and I agree on this matter, we are likely to lose this battle. Sentences like those above with "sat" sounds odd to people of a certain age, but they are in common use.

There are other changes underway with respect to the use of prepositions or types of objects allowed with a particular verb. I quite often find that my students can use the verb *discuss* with a following sentential sentence argument— *they discussed that* ....

> The sentence "We discuss that the software enhances the clarity and flow of complex ideas." is grammatically incorrect. Here is how I would suggest revising it:

"We discuss how the software enhances the clarity and flow of complex ideas."
The main issue is the use of "that" after the verb "discuss". The verb "discuss" needs to be followed by a noun clause, usually introduced by "how", "what", "whether" etc.
Using "that" here is incorrect, as "that" is used to introduce a noun clause after verbs like "say", "think", "believe", but not usually after "discuss".
The revision using "how" creates a grammatically correct noun clause that properly follows the main verb "discuss".
Other ways to fix it would be:
"We discuss the way the software enhances the clarity and flow of complex ideas."
Or
"Our discussion focuses on how the software enhances the clarity and flow of complex ideas."
By changing the noun clause structure and using more appropriate connecting words like "how", "the way", the sentence can be corrected.

It is interesting that Claude says that *discuss* does not 'usually' take a following *that*-clause, which suggests that Claude has, in fact, come across that usage a few times in the training data.

A rather different use of Claude is to help us understand the finer points of grammar related to synonyms and other subtle distinctions in meaning. There are many instances of semantic distinctions that we can perceive but not quite put a finger on. Examples might include synonyms for pairs of sentences such as *I met John* and *I met with John.* Could you explain the difference? We can ask Claude for an explanation .

The main difference between "I met John" and "I met with John" is:
"I met John" implies a brief, chance encounter with John. This focuses on the act of meeting itself.
For example:
I met John at the store yesterday.
I met John once at a party years ago.
"I met with John" implies a planned, intentional meeting with John. This focuses on having a full interaction.
For example:
I met with John to discuss the project.
I met with John for lunch to catch up.

I met with John and the rest of the team.
Some key differences:
"Met with" suggests a more substantive, intentional meeting, while "met" can mean a quick unplanned encounter.
"Met with" works for scheduled meetings, "met" for chance meetings.
"Met with" implies you spent time interacting, while "met" simply means you encountered them.
"Met with" is used for meetings on a shared topic or purpose, "met" is more general.
So in summary, "met with" indicates a planned, purposeful meeting, while "met" can mean a brief, casual encounter. The context the sentence provides determines the right usage.

First prompts

We have seen how Claude revises sample texts and how it responds to specific grammatical questions. I suggest that you try writing some prompts to evaluate the grammatical correctness of your writing. You can ask direct questions. Here are some examples.

Is the following correct.
Which is better, X or Y?
What tense should I use in the Literature Review of an article?
What is the subjunctive?
List any errors in the text.
List the improvements you would make to the text.

You should add context to the above prompts. The context might be very general—I am a linguist writing a research article—or something related to discourse, such as I am working on the first sentence of an essay.

If you are not sure how to proceed to get the best response, you can engage with the AI Assistant about the responses that are likely to get the best results. Here is my prompt: How do I construct prompts that will help you help me with my writing? I am a linguist writing a research article. The AI Assistant provides some useful suggestions.

Here are some suggestions for constructing effective prompts for me to help with your writing:
1. Be specific about the part of your writing you need help with.
For example:
Proofreading for grammatical errors

Improving clarity or flow in a section of text
Generating ideas for a particular section or argument
Organizing and structuring your paper
2. Provide the relevant context and background. Give me some information about:
The general topic or research question of your article
The purpose, audience, and genre of your writing
Any specific instructions or requirements from editors or reviewers
3. Outline the key points you want to make in the section of writing. This helps me understand the concepts and arguments you want to convey.
4. Share any instructions or feedback you've already received from reviewers or editors. This ensures I'm helping you address any issues they've identified.
5. Ask specific, clear questions about the part you need help with. For example:
Does this paragraph clearly introduce the research question?
How could I strengthen this argument?
Are my instructions to participants clearly explained?
6. Provide relevant extracts of your writing for me to review. The more context and material I have, the more targeted help I can provide.
7. Be available to answer any clarifying questions I have. My suggestions will be most useful if I fully understand your research, writing goals and needs.
Does this help? Let me know if you have any other questions. I'd be happy to recommend any additional strategies for getting the help you need with your research article writing.

We are not used to getting this level of support. Once we graduate from university, it is difficult to find someone willing to read and comment on our efforts at writing. Having an AI Assistant at hand is going to be very valuable in supporting our writing. It is too early to see where this is going to take us, but the onus is clearly on the human writer to think critically and purposefully about the content and aims of the writing in order to maximize the value of the human-AI collaboration.

Stay critical

Let me emphasise again that it is very important not to assume that the response from Claude is correct. If you have doubts, you can follow up and ask whether Claude is sure about a grammatical point. Or, you can ask for further details or alternatives. When you are first using an AI Assistant, it will help you in longer term if you learn to follow up on the response in some way. You can challenge the response; you can say that it is too general or too superficial. Or you can tell Claude that you are an English teacher and ask for a response appropriate for your role. And again, if you have any doubts, you can probe more deeply. As a practical point, note that the revised or elaborated output from Claude tends to be better than the first pass at responding. You sometimes need to engage in a dialogue, as you would with a co-author.

Bread and jam again

To return to the bread and jam example, I asked Claude whether it was absolutely sure that bread and jam in subject position took a plural verb. The response was quite nuanced.

> In the case of "bread and jam," I believe it is less common to think of this food pairing as a fixed singular unit. "Bread and butter" is a more set phrase. So I would still recommend using a plural verb for "bread and jam" in most cases:
> "Bread and jam are my favorite snack."
> But I appreciate you pointing this out - it's a good reminder that compound subjects can be tricky, and sometimes singular/plural verb use depends on whether the subject is considered a single unit or separate items.

Personally, I can do without the false claim of some 'appreciation.'

I also challenged Claude concerning a suggested change in the tense in one of the pieces of writing that I wanted Claude to evaluate.

> Upon further reflection, I believe my original suggestion of changing "were" to "had been" is incorrect. Here's my updated thinking ....

I am not sure whether this is magical or surreal. I am amazed that I can get Claude to focus on and reassess a particular issue. However, it is important to note that this reassessment is part of the interface. The underlying GPT has input and output; there is nothing equivalent to reflection.

The examples in this chapter highlight some issues related to cultural norms and the fallibility of Claude in correctly assessing some grammatical points. In general, Claude is better at writing or rewriting chunks of text than at giving examples and analysis. Most of the time the information given by the AI is excellent. Here, rather than illustrating all aspects of grammatical help offered by Claude, I have focused on areas where I suspected there might be some weakness.

4 Improve Your Writing

Two important elements of strong writing are being clear and concise. Claude states that writing should clearly communicate the writer's exact ideas and message to the reader. It should also be concise by removing any unnecessary words and repetition. The notion is that this improves readability and keeps the reader's attention focused.

Claude's is able to help in this regard by
* Identifying Wordy or Vague Phrases
* Simplifying Sentence Structure
* Reducing Unnecessary Filler Words
* Shortening Rambling Sentences
* Eliminating Redundancies
* Condensing To Communicate More With Less

Claude claims to sharpen your writing is by flagging any vague or wordy phrases that sound good, but don't communicate any concrete meaning. For instance, Claude gives the following example.

Wordy: *The financial prognosis indicates decreased fiscal viability.*
Clear: *We are losing money.*

As you can see, this is not right. The revised version is concise, but the tone or genre is too different from the original. The example illustrates Claude ability to identify wordy or vague phrases. The problem comes in the form of the suggested revision.

The example above was produced by Claude to illustrate the kind of revisions it might suggest. When I explicitly asked Claude to revise the wordy sentence—*The financial prognosis indicates decreased fiscal viability*—the actual responses were much better:

> Suggestions:
> *Our financial forecast shows lower profitability.*
> *The financial outlook predicts worsening financial health.*
> *Our budget predicts declining monetary sustainability.*
> *Financial projections point to worsening economic feasibility.*
> *Analyses indicate decreasing financial stability for the company.*

These responses are pretty good. It is interesting that Claude is better at doing a task than describing doing a task, an observation we will explore further towards the end of the chapter.

Simplifying sentence structure

Long, convoluted sentences can easily lose the reader. To help with this, Claude will identify any complex sentences and suggest splitting them into two or more sentences for simplicity. If you query Claude about a complex sentence you have written, Claude will nearly always make some changes. Here is an example.

> Here are a few suggestions to improve the clarity and readability of this sentence:
> **Original:**
> *We consider the nature of the fit between particular theoretical approaches and the three areas in which corpus linguistics has made a significant contribution to our understanding of language: the provision of frequency information, the highlighting of the importance of collocations, and the description of variation and text types.*
> ***Suggested revisions:***
> 1. *We examine how well different theoretical approaches align with the three major areas where corpus linguistics has significantly furthered our understanding of language. These areas are: providing frequency data, emphasizing the importance of collocations, and describing variation across text types.*

2. *We evaluate how compatible specific theoretical frameworks are with the three main contributions of corpus linguistics to the study of language. These contributions include supplying frequency information, highlighting collocation patterns, and delineating variation between text types.*

The key changes:

Split one long sentence into two for better readability

Simplified wording like "examine" instead of "consider the nature"

Removed passive voice ("has been made") for clarity

Explained the three areas briefly rather than just listing

Used "major/main" instead of "significant" for concision

Changed "our understanding" to "the study" for precision

The revisions aim to make the sentence more straightforward by streamlining wordiness, using active voice, explaining the key points briefly, and improving sentence structure. This enhances the clarity and flow of the complex ideas.

Are the changes an improvement? I prefer revision 1 over revision 2. What is particularly useful is the listing of the potential changes by the AI Assistant. So, rather than taking the revised paragraph and pasting it into a document, we can look at the suggested revisions and see which ones we believe improve the writing.

The AI Assistant will always make some suggestions and make some revisions to your writing. Here is another example.

The sentence is mostly grammatically correct, but could be improved for clarity and concision:

Original:

This section introduces some basic issues concerning the treatment of theory and data in corpus linguistics and outlines three broad areas in which corpus linguistics has made a significant contribution to our understanding of the nature of language.

Suggested revision:

This section covers basic issues around theory and data in corpus linguistics. It also outlines three major areas where corpus linguistics has significantly furthered understanding of language.

Changes made:

Shortened introduction clause for concision

Replaced "outlines" with more direct "covers"

Removed passive voice ("has been made") for clarity

Replaced "our understanding" with "understanding" for simplicity

Changed "significant contribution" to "significantly furthered" for brevity

Removed "the nature of" as unnecessary wordiness

Overall, the original is grammatically valid but could be tightened up through word choice simplification, passive voice removal, and reducing redundant phrasing. The revised version communicates the key ideas more clearly and concisely.

What do you think about the suggested revision? There is no doubt that the revised text is clear and concise. Personally, in this instance, I would not split the text into two sentences. The original sentence is not going to cause problems for an academic reader. And here we get into considerations such as style and rhythm, and also personal preferences. We need some variety in sentence patterns and sentence length. Does Claude take note of that?

What we can say is that we all have our personal preferences and our own style; we don't want that to be overridden by our AI Assistants.

Style

I asked Claude to write a paragraph on AI. Here is the response..

> As artificial intelligence progresses, advanced writing technologies promise to aid authors in profound new ways. However, realizing the full potential of this collaboration requires thoughtful participation by the human partners involved. By reflecting on our own strengths, weaknesses, and objectives, we can guide technology to fill gaps rather than replace talents.

The sentences are all more or less the same length (and each sentence consists of a subordinate and main clause). This is a subtle observation, but this uniformity will have an effect on how we perceive the writing. Having noticed this uniformity, I can ask Claude to change the writing to make it more varied in terms of sentence length.

> As artificial intelligence progresses, advanced writing technologies promise to aid authors in profound new ways. However, realizing the full potential of this human-AI collaboration will require thoughtful participation by the people involved. We humans must reflect on our own strengths, weaknesses, and goals. That way, we can guide technology to fill gaps rather than replace talents. If we approach

> this partnership thoughtfully, AI can complement what we do best - bringing creativity, emotion, and meaning to the written word. But we must reflect carefully on how to combine our unique abilities with advanced algorithms. By considering our objectives and abilities, we can direct technology to enhance human expression, not replace it.

The AI Assistant seems to have added shorter sentences consisting only of a main clause to add variability. The revised version does not read particularly well. It may be that being based on a word prediction model leads Claude to generate sentences of a certain length.

Will AI lead to changes in the structure of discourse such that writing styles converge on the preferred style of the AI Assistants? My sense is that Claude's preference for shorter sentences throughout a paragraph leads to a very choppy style. However, after some time, that might be how we all write and what readers expect. And what I see as choppy may be viewed by some readers and writers as helping to maintain interest or attention.

More revisions

Look at the following sentence (or better yet use a sentence you have written). Underline the parts that you think Claude will change.

> *Now that corpus linguistics been widely used in linguistic analyses, we can look for the conceptual links between corpus data and theoretical approaches within a broad swath of linguistic traditions.*

Since I wrote (and revised) the sentence, it is hard for me to see how to improve it. Claude suggested the following revision.

> Corpus linguistics is now widely used in linguistic analyses, allowing us to explore conceptual links between corpus data and theoretical approaches across a broad range of linguistic traditions.

I have to admit to being a little disheartened by how good the revision is. My disappointment led me to remember a scene in David Lodge's novel *Changing Places* in which the famous writer Morris Zapp is told what word he uses frequently.

> *"The computer has counted and tabulated the words in the different books and articles you have published over the last ten years. It finds*

that your favorite adjective, the word that occurs more frequently than any other qualifying word in your writing, is the word 'euphoric'."

At first Morris was amused by this. Unfortunately, later this knowledge led him to suffer from writer's block. He was stuck because his prose continually led him to the point of using the word *euphoric*, which he wanted to avoid since he had learned he was overusing it. However, he couldn't come up with any alternative wording and, in the end, couldn't finish his manuscript on Milton.

I am just wondering whether my suspicion that the AI assistant can write better than me will actually hinder my willingness to write in the future.

To digress for a moment. I thought about the scene from *Changing Places*, but wasn't sure of the details. I tried looking for it on Google books, but the novel is not available there. I turned to Claude and asked whether there was a scene in a David Lodge novel in which a writer is informed what his favourite adjective is. Claude said it couldn't help. Did I know the title of the novel? I guessed *Changing Places* and Claude immediately found and explained the scene. I followed up to confirm that after this episode Morris couldn't continue with his manuscript. Again, Claude found quotes and described the outcome.

Fillers

Getting back to the use of precise language, one aim of the software is to reduce unnecessary filler words. According to Claude, filler words like *basically, obviously, just, actually,* and *you see* clutter sentences without adding additional meaning. Claude highlights these fillers for removal.

Original: I'm actually not really clear on the direction they want to take with the new branding.
Revised: I'm unclear on the direction they want to take with the new branding.

In this example from Claude, the revised version is clear and concise. We all write things like *actually not really* in our emails and sometimes there is a good reason to do this. We may want to express some uncertainty or adopt a tentative tone, especially if we are being somewhat critical of the person we are addressing.

In general, when you see Claude highlight a potential redundancy, double check if it actually adds pragmatic value rather than just obscures the main idea. Eliminate it if it does not provide any meaningful addition to the sentence. Here is the advice from Claude.

> Try out Claude's condensing suggestions for long sections of your writing. Identify techniques it uses, such as focusing on key details, using concise phrasing, and removing expendable elaboration. Practice condensing content yourself. While you may not want to trim as extremely as Claude does, it builds skills in streamlining your communication. By using Claude's analysis and feedback on clarity and concision, you can train yourself to write in a more clear, direct, and succinct style. Your writing will become tighter and more effective at communicating your true intent to readers. Concision does require eliminating thoughts that seem valuable but ultimately clutter your central message and point. This takes practice, but continuous use of Claude will build your concision abilities. Your readers will appreciate writing that is clear, focused, and does not waste their time.

Word choice

Claude lists the following ways to improve word choice and style.

* Replacing Overused Words with Stronger Alternatives
* Improving Vague Verbs with Specific Action Words
* Eliminating Unnecessary Adverbs and Adjectives
* Using Descriptive Words That Evoke Imagery
* Matching Word Choice to Your Intended Tone
* Fixing Repetition and Redundancies
* Expanding Sentences With Phrasal Verbs
* Practicing Concision Through Compression

* Applying Figurative Language and Rhetorical Devices
* Developing Your Distinct Writing Voice

One of the suggestions is using phrasal verbs expand your vocabulary and style.

For instance:
Original: The company started the new project.
Claude's suggestion: The company rolled out the new project.

The idea, according to the software, is that phrasal verbs like *rolled out* are more descriptive and lively compared to basic verbs like *started.* That is interesting. Phrasal verbs can 'lighten' writing, but the choice of phrasal verb is closely tied to the particular genre of the writing and so it can be difficult to get the right tone. I asked Claude whether the following was a good sentence – *The researchers got rid of the outlier data points.*

Yes, that is a grammatically correct and clearly written sentence. Here are a few notes on why it is effective:

It uses the active voice ("The researchers got rid of..."), which emphasizes the researchers as the ones performing the action. This makes the sentence straightforward and easy to understand.

The verb "got rid of" clearly conveys the action being described. Alternative phrasings like "eliminated" or "excluded" could work too, but "got rid of" is informal enough for a general audience while still being technically accurate.

The object "the outlier data points" is concise yet descriptive. It's clear what specifically the researchers removed without additional verbose explanation needed.

The sentence structure is simple and follows a clear subject-verb-object format. There are no convoluted clauses or confusing arrangements.

It avoids extraneous adverbs or adjectives that aren't strictly necessary. The meaning is very transparent without them.

Overall, the sentence succinctly and clearly conveys the action being described in an easy-to-understand way. The active voice, solid verb choice, and simple but effective language make it an effective, well-constructed sentence.

I thought that the words *researcher* and *data outlier* would indicate that this was a sentence from an academic text and that *get rid of* is not appropriate. Apparently, the context is too small for Claude to detect that the sentence was written in an academic style. However, when I asked explicitly whether the sentence was appropriate for academic writing, the response was:

> No, the sentence "The researchers got rid of the outlier data points" does not have an appropriate tone for formal academic writing. Here are a few suggestions to improve the tone:
>
> Avoid informal phrasing like "got rid of." More formal alternatives would be "excluded," "omitted," or "removed."
>
> Add more specificity on why the outliers were removed and how: "The researchers excluded the outlier data points from the analysis to avoid skewing the results."
>
> Use technical language suited for academic discourse: "The researchers eliminated the statistical outliers from the dataset to preclude aberrant values from distorting the analysis."
>
> Maintain objectivity with a declarative tone: "Outlier data points were excluded by the research team to prevent anomalous values from introducing bias."
>
> Cite a source if referring to standard outlier removal practices: "As is common practice (Jones et al. 2019), outlier data points exceeding 2 standard deviations from the mean were omitted by the researchers prior to analysis."
>
> The original phrasing "got rid of" is too informal and vague for scholarly writing. Adjusting the word choice, adding more detail, using technical language, maintaining an objective tone, and citing sources for such procedural steps would elevate the sentence to have appropriate academic style. Precision, formality, and objectivity are key considerations when writing for scholarly audiences.

This illustrates some potential dangers of working with phrases or single sentences rather than with larger texts when asking about genre.

Academic "we"

Let's test Claude and see what the response is to the somewhat controversial use of self-mentions such as "we" in academic writing.

> The use of "we" in academic writing is a complex issue with perspectives on both sides, but here is a summary of guidelines:

> Using "we" is generally acceptable in most academic disciplines, especially in the introduction or methods sections when describing actions the author(s) took.
>
> However, some fields like the humanities prefer avoiding "we" in favor of passive voice or third person (e.g., "This paper investigates..." or "The authors investigated...").
>
> Overusing "we" can sound too informal. It should be used strategically and sparingly.
>
> Avoid ambiguous or unclear uses of "we" - make sure it refers specifically to the authors. Using "we" to refer to society/humanity can cause confusion.
>
> Do not use "we" to make unjustified overgeneralizations or overstate conclusions. Stick to actions the authors themselves performed.
>
> Use "we" mainly for describing the current paper rather than universal claims. For general statements, passive voice is safer.
>
> So in the example sentence, the use of "we investigate" is perfectly acceptable since it describes the action taken in this specific paper. But "we" should be employed judiciously overall in academic writing, depending on disciplinary conventions. The alternatives of rephrasing in the passive voice or using "this paper" also work if the author wants to avoid "we" entirely.

The summary is useful and reasonable and the point about only using *we* to refer to the authors is clearly a good one. The use of *we* to refer to the author and reader, as in *we see that* is not mentioned, although it is a relatively common usage.

Pride and Prejudice

I tried to trick Claude by giving it the famous opening sentence of Jane Austen's Pride and Prejudice. *It is a truth universally acknowledged, that a single man in possession of a good fortune, must be in want of a wife.* I thought the software might try to convert it to something plainer. But no,

> Yes, this is a very well-constructed and famous sentence:
>
> "It is a truth universally acknowledged, that a single man in possession of a good fortune, must be in want of a wife."
>
> This sentence opens Jane Austen's novel Pride and Prejudice (1813).
>
> Here's an analysis of why it's effective:

It establishes the major theme and conflict of the story (marriage, courtship, money) right from the start.
The diction is sophisticated and reflective of Austen's era ("universally acknowledged," "in possession of a good fortune").
It uses the rhetorical devices of parallelism ("a single man in possession...") and epistrophe ("of a good fortune, must be...") to create a lyrical, memorable opening.
The emphasis on "single man" and "wife" hooks the reader and hints at the plot involving courtship and marital dynamics.

The sentence has a timeless quality and unveils an "undeniable truth" about Austen's society regarding marriage and money. Overall, this is considered an extremely well-crafted, impactful opening line that effectively sets the tone, themes, and premises of the novel. The sentence holds up beautifully over 200 years later as a masterwork of English prose. So in summary, yes it is a very good, artfully composed sentence!

Implicit versus explicit knowledge.

We all have implicit knowledge of our mother tongue. We know the proper usage of thousands of words; the structure of utterances or sentences; how to use language appropriately to achieve different ends: how to apologise, how to make suggestions, and so on. We do this more or less effortlessly and without thinking about how we do it. That is true most of the time, though there may be situations where we have to choose our words carefully and we pay more attention to what we are saying. All that automatic activity comes from implicit knowledge of our first language. We don't really know how we do it, we just do it. Another way of talking about it is to say that we cannot directly access the implicit knowledge about language that we make use of, though we can always make up a story about what we know.

What about explicit knowledge of language? This comes into play when we were doing a crossword or playing Wordle and have to think of a five-letter word beginning with S and ending in P. Another situation might be where we are teaching a language or someone ask us a question about language. For instance, should I say *if I was rich* or *if I were rich*? In answering this question, you may well not know which form you use. You may say that the answer is *if I were rich* because that is what you were taught. It may be that what you actually say in conversation is *if I was rich*. In this case, you would be using explicit knowledge for the response to a question and implicit knowledge when speaking naturally.

It is interesting that Claude acts in a way that suggests it has a similar kind of distinction. In other words, like a person who is asked a question about language, the software gives one answer when being explicit about usage and may give another kind of response when simply generating the language. It seems that Claude can analyse texts and can write texts, but sometimes has difficulty with some explicit tasks. This highlights the fact that Claude is not looking up answers in a database. It is a word prediction model. It can answer questions and can produce coherent text. It can't do some simple analytical tasks as illustrated below.

> List the prepositions in the following text:
> It is interesting that Claude acts in a way that suggests it has a similar kind of distinction. In other words, like a person who is asked a question about language, the software gives one answer when being explicit about usage and may give another kind of response when simply generating the language
>
> Here are the prepositions I identified in the given text:
> in - "It is interesting that Claude acts in a way that suggests"
> in - "In other words, like a "
> about - "who is asked a question about language,"
> when - "gives one answer when being explicit about usage,"
> when - "may give another kind of response when simply generating the language"
> So there are 5 distinct prepositions used in the text:
> in
> about
> when
> like
> with

What does this mean when using Claude? I am not entirely sure. It is certainly useful to ask Claude direct questions about usage. Just be aware that the output may be better when Claude is simply creating language in response to your prompt.

Expanding your writing

One of the most useful features of Claude's AI capabilities is its ability to analyse your writing and offer suggestions to expand, elaborate, and enrich your ideas. Claude can play a role in providing new angles, insights, and directions to pursue. Claude suggests techniques such as:

* Asking Claude Direct Questions
* Generating Supporting Examples
* Providing Definitions and Explanations
* Adding Counterpoints and Opposing Views
* Identifying Missing Context and Background
* Summarizing Lengthy Content
* Making Explicit Implications and Inferences
* Offering Alternative Titles/Headings
* Rewriting From Different Perspectives
* Researching Facts and Sources
* Condensing Ideas Sharply
* Inserting Rhetorical Questions

Generating content

We have covered direct questions about the formal aspects of writing. You can also ask about content. An example could be something simple like: *What are some potential advantages of adopting this proposal?* Or, *what are some arguments against the proposal and how can they be countered?*

Clearly, we are stepping over a line here. We are not asking for help with the form of writing; we are asking for assistance with the content. Taking this step made me a little uneasy, at first. However, this is the new reality. This is how we are working and I believe that it will be the norm. It did not take me long to accept the use of AI as an idea-generator. It is so easy to ask for 10 or 20 ideas/topics and select the best ones to develop or use from the list to spark your own creativity. I would do this when preparing topics for a new course, but I wouldn't ask for this assistance with content in my professional academic writing. If a future AI had the ability to suggest ways to make a new contribution to the field, I personally would resist that. I am not taking a moral standpoint. One reason is that a new contribution would be diminished in my estimation if it weren't my own. (I have to admit that this viewpoint is somewhat naïve since my 'own' contributions would be influenced by the work of others.) More germane is the fact that I am not a young researcher seeking to make an impact and further my career. I am not under pressure to write a book to get tenure, for instance. The resistance relates to my identity as a researcher. I have no qualms about making substantial use of AI in generating topics in the writing of this book. The initial topics came from Claude. I started by selecting some of these topics and followed the themes and added my responses to the output of Claude. As I explored those topics, I added my own as I thought about what might be some consequences of having access to AI tools for students and teachers.

Institutional responses

This is my personal response. The question then becomes how we respond to this at an institutional level. What is the policy in schools and colleges about using and citing AI Assistants? It's going to be very complicated since, as with all work with a co-author, it is difficult to tell when looking at the finished product who contributed what. How will guidelines be enforced or checked? In my assignments this year, I have tried a couple of things. In one instance I gave the whole class the prompt and response relevant to the assignment and told the class not to try any further prompts. In another class, I made assessment of the output of relevant prompts a part of the assignment. I have seen some institutions try to draw a line between licit and illicit use of AI. The policy of some UK universities includes the following:

> Universities will support students and staff to become AI-literate.

Staff should be equipped to support students to use generative AI tools effectively and appropriately in their learning experience.

Universities will adapt teaching and assessment to incorporate the ethical use of generative AI and support equal access.

Universities will ensure academic rigour and integrity is upheld.

The proposal states that academic rigour and integrity will be upheld by having clear policies on what is acceptable practice and what is not. We will have to see how guidelines evolve over the next few years. At present, some of the recommendations I have seen are trying to make a distinction between AI-assisted and AI-generated writing. The idea is that it is acceptable to ask for topics and ideas; it is not appropriate to use AI to write an assignment. Here is an example from one university:

AI-allowed

Get a general overview of your topic before you begin researching in more detail

Help you to improve your writing skills, including grammar, use of vocabulary, and sentence structure

AI-disallowed

Using AI to write or develop your assessments for you. All work that you submit must be your own work and representative of your capabilities.

We will see how practices and recommendations develop over the next few years. We might need AI to oversee our AI use.

5 Writing a Research Paper

AI can be used to aid all aspects of writing. This is the current reality. There may be some AI systems that do not presently connect to the internet, but if there are then that will change very soon and AI Assistants will have access to all the resources of the internet. Claude is able to access the internet.

It should be clear from what we have covered in this book that getting a substantial amount of help to write an assignment, in terms of both the content and the writing, is very straightforward in a technical sense. Let us explore this in practical terms by writing a research paper. I hesitate in doing this, but it important that we are all aware of the capabilities of the software. The aim is to show what is possible; I am definitely not suggesting that this is an acceptable way to write a research paper.

Paper topic

We need to first come up with at least a vague idea of what to work on. I opted for 'individual differences in language use among ESL learners.'

Here is a suggested research topic on individual differences in language usage among ESL (English as a Second Language) learners: "Examining the relationship between personality traits and lexical diversity in ESL learners' spoken English"

Key points about this suggested topic:

Focuses on individual differences in ESL learners' spoken vocabulary usage based on their personality traits.

Lexical diversity refers to the variety and sophistication of vocabulary used. The hypothesis could be that certain personality traits (e.g. extraversion, openness) correlate with higher lexical diversity.

Spoken vocabulary is chosen as oral fluency and vocabulary usage may relate more to ingrained personality traits versus written work.

The study could survey ESL learners to classify their personality traits and then analyze speeches/conversations for lexical diversity metrics like VOC-D, MTLD, HD-D/VS to compare.

Results could provide insights on the relationship between innate student characteristics and oral vocabulary capabilities and have implications for adaptive ESL teaching.

Let me know if you would like me to expand on this suggested topic or propose alternative research ideas related to individual language differences in ESL learners. I'm happy to brainstorm further ideas and specifics to help

This is a possibility to consider; I asked for another suggestion for a specific topic.

Here's another suggested research topic on individual differences in ESL learners' language use:

"Investigating the effects of learning style preferences on English vocabulary acquisition strategies in ESL students"

Key details:

Focuses on whether different learning styles (visual, auditory, reading/writing, kinesthetic) affect how ESL students best acquire new English vocabulary.

Learning styles could be assessed through questionnaires. Vocabulary acquisition strategies could be measured through surveys, interviews, and vocabulary tests.

Strategies could include repetition, associating words with images, taking notes, using flashcards, listening to vocabulary tapes, etc.

The hypothesis is that certain vocabulary acquisition strategies will be more effective depending on an individual's learning style preferences.

Results could lead to customized vocabulary instruction approaches adapted to students' learning styles.

Let me know if you would like me to propose another potential research topic or expand on this suggestion further. I'm happy to keep discussing possibilities to help develop a fruitful research question!

I prefer the first option; I am pretty certain that a lot of research has been carried out on learning style. I then ask for a 150-word abstract for the first topic Claude suggested the following.

Here is a 150 word abstract for the research proposal:

This quantitative study investigates connections between ESL learners' personality traits and lexical diversity in their spoken English. Lexical diversity refers to sophistication of vocabulary. Participants will complete Big Five personality inventories and recorded speaking tasks. Their speech samples will be analyzed using metrics like VOCD and MTLD to quantify lexical diversity features including word types, frequencies and redundancy. Regression analyses will identify if personality traits predict lexical diversity when controlling for other variables. It's hypothesized openness and extraversion will positively correlate with lexical diversity given their associations with verbal fluency. However, conscientiousness may relate to use of more common words. Examining these relationships provides empirical evidence on how personality tendencies manifest in vocabulary usage. Findings may inform adaptations to ESL pedagogy based on learner personalities. This study focuses on diversity in spoken vocabulary across personality spectra to yield key insights on individual differences influencing core language development.

Of course, the abstract would need to be edited. However, I want Claude to change the content a little because I found from a web search that there is some free software, TAALES, that automatically measures lexical sophistication. I told the AI Assistant to rewrite the abstract to incorporate the use of this tool.

This quantitative study investigates connections between ESL learners' personality traits and lexical sophistication in their spoken English. Lexical sophistication refers to the use of advanced vocabulary. Participants will complete Big Five personality inventories and recorded speaking tasks. Their speech samples will be analyzed using TAALES to measure lexical sophistication features including word rareness, specificity, and difficulty. TAALES provides text analysis based on corpora word frequencies. Regression analyses will identify if personality traits predict TAALES lexical sophistication scores when controlling for covariates. It's hypothesized openness and extraversion will correlate positively with lexical sophistication given verbal fluency associations. However, conscientiousness may relate to use of simpler vocabulary. Analyzing these relationships provides empirical evidence on how personality tendencies manifest in sophisticated word choice. Findings can inform adaptations to ESL teaching based on learner personalities. Focusing on TAALES-measured lexical sophistication will yield insights on individual differences driving vocabulary usage.

Let me reiterate that I am showing the unedited versions of the responses from the AI. We can direct the software to rewrite any parts we don't like before starting to make revisions manually.

The Introduction

I could ask Claude to search for relevant citations. In this case, I carried out a quick search myself and retrieved a few relevant references and then told the AI to write an introduction taking account of those references.

> Individual learner differences have been shown to influence second language acquisition outcomes across linguistic domains (Ackerman, 1994; 1999). Specifically, personality traits measured through frameworks like the Big Five and Myers-Briggs have demonstrated relationships with varied language proficiency and usage patterns (Carrell et al., 1996; Chan & Eysenck, 1981; Ehrman & Oxford, 1990). However, few studies have focused on how personality correlates to vocabulary proficiency. As vocabulary size and sophistication are vital to overall second language mastery (Briggs Myers et al., 1998), this research aims to elucidate connections between personality traits and lexical sophistication in ESL learners' speech. Using the Big Five inventory and TAALES text analysis of recorded samples, it examines whether certain traits relate to usage of advanced vocabulary. Identifying these relationships can enhance pedagogical approaches, like adapting methods to learners' personalities (Geisler-Brenstein & Schmeck, 1996; Goh & Moore, 1987). This empirical investigation of personality and lexical proficiency will provide key insights on individual differences influencing core language acquisition.

I am not sure that the citations are all in the right place. It looks reasonable. It is not very long. I could ask for a longer version.

AI detection

On a side note, even though I added the research articles, this text is likely to be detected as AI-generated. You can ask Claude to write in a way that avoids AI-detection. I don't recommend that due to ethical concerns and due to the fact that when I generated the no-detection version, it was not as good in terms of style and content. And when I tested the revised version, it was still flagged as AI-generated.

After I spent a few minutes making very minor improvements in the wording, the AI detection score dropped from 100% to 43%. I only made some small changes at the word/phrase level.

Method section

Next is the Methodology section. I didn't give Claude any guidelines; I just asked it to write up the methodology for the study. To 'carry out' this research, we need to assess the personality of the students and measure the lexical sophistication of their language production.

> Here is a 150 word methodology section:
> This study will utilize a quantitative approach to assess the relationship between personality traits and lexical sophistication. Participants will include 100 adult ESL learners with intermediate English proficiency recruited from language programs. Personality will be measured using the Big Five Inventory questionnaire with subscales for extraversion, agreeableness, conscientiousness, neuroticism, and openness. Participants will also complete a 3-minute videotaped speaking task on daily routines to elicit natural language samples. Speech recordings will be transcribed and analyzed using the TAALES text analysis tool to generate lexical sophistication scores including word frequency ranks, word rareness, and word ambiguity. Higher TAALES scores indicate usage of advanced vocabulary. Transcripts will also be analyzed for total words to control for sample size effects. Multiple regression analysis will then determine if Big Five personality traits significantly predict TAALES lexical sophistication scores when controlling for confounding variables like age, gender, and education. This meth-

odology provides empirical examination of relationships between personality and advanced vocabulary usage patterns.

Again, we could ask for a more detailed description. You could break down the section into different components and ask for an elaborated description of each one. This is a good general technique if you are constructing a large text or you simply want more detailed responses.

Results section

For the next stage we would have to actually do the research. However, for the purposes of this illustration, I asked Claude to 'imagine' the results.

> Here is an imagined 150-word results section for this experiment: Multiple regression analysis revealed personality traits as significant predictors of lexical sophistication ($F=2.51$, $p<.05$, $R2=.17$). Extraversion positively correlated with TAALES scores ($\beta=.25$, $t=2.1$, $p=.03$), suggesting more outgoing personalities use advanced vocabulary. Openness also showed a positive relationship ($\beta=.20$, $t=1.8$, $p=.04$). In contrast, conscientiousness negatively associated with lexical sophistication ($\beta=-.29$, $t=-2.5$, $p=.01$), indicating use of simpler vocabulary among more rule-abiding individuals. Figure 1 illustrates these correlations. Agreeableness and neuroticism did not significantly correlate with lexical sophistication. Overall, the Big Five traits explained 17% of variance in TAALES scores when controlling for length, age, gender, and education. These findings provide initial evidence that innate personality differences manifest in ESL learners' lexical proficiency. Further research can expand on these relationships to tailor vocabulary instruction to student personalities.

Not surprisingly, the imagined results is the weakest section.

Writing in academia

We don't need to go any further with this research article. We have shown that with the absolute minimum of human intervention, we can put together a research paper. If we engaged with the content more closely, and provided more input, then we may be able to produce a reasonably 'good' research article—i.e., publishable somewhere. It would be interesting to see what happened if I submitted this article to a third tier journal. Hopefully, it would not be accepted.

I have illustrated the easiest method of creating a research article, which is based on asking the AI to generate the content. All I did was search for a few references. This is clearly a radical departure from normal practice. It would be even more egregious if I adopted a more unethical strategy such as inputting the Introductions from four or five articles on the same topic and asking Claude to make use of those in writing the introduction on 'my' research topic. Another dubious alternative would be to give Claude the URLs of relevant papers and ask for a summary.

What all this means for academia and academic publishing, I am not sure. Will we have an appendix in research articles that lists all the prompts we have used in producing the paper? I don't know. The problems will be particularly acute in the short-term as we face a combination of rapid progress in the development and uptake of AI systems combined with the slow development of meaningful guidelines by the affected institutions.

6 Prompt Engineering

Prompt engineering is a rather grand term for the description of different options for interacting with AI Assistants. While the previous chapters covered core features of Claude for improving writing, getting to a level of skilled use requires learning some advanced techniques as well. By now, you will have a good sense of the capabilities of Claude and the kinds of task that Claude can carry out. The aim now is to make sure you can get the best response from Claude.

Turn taking

One way of interacting with Claude is similar to having a conversation. You might pose a simple prompt and then follow-up on the response with further prompts to elaborate on certain points, get a more sophisticated response, or simply follow a line of inquiry, just as you would if you were having a dialogue with an expert. One answer might naturally lead to another question.

Once Claude has provided a response to a prompt, you might simply want to ask for more information. Here is a simple list to illustrate some examples of follow-up prompts.

Expand on why you thought this section was unclear
Your response is very general, be more specific
I am a linguist, give a more sophisticated response
Give a specific example to illustrate this principle
Describe how your suggested rewrite strengthens the original phrasing
Rewrite this in a more informal, conversational tone
Provide an integrated rewrite of this section incorporating your advice to add details, improve clarity, and enhance flow
Generate an original metaphor to illustrate this idea
I don't agree with your proposed revision. Explain why you made this suggestion and the reasoning behind it

The three main strategies in prompt engineering can be boiled down to (i) using targeted follow-up prompts. (ii) adding as much context and detail to the prompt as possible and (iii) asking Claude to help construct a prompt. New users of AI Assistants will probably start off using prompts similar to those used in Google. However, it will not take long before they are chatting back and forth with the AI.

Some parts of this chapter might seem a little technical and perhaps even somewhat boring. You might scan through the chapter for now, and then later use the index to search for specific techniques or formats that are useful for you.

Overview of functions

Let us first review the different types of action the AI can carry out on a text.

Extraction operations

Provide summaries: (e.g., summarise the following text in 100 words.)

Extract specific information: (e.g., list the errors in the following text)

Analyse data: (e.g., list the moves/steps in the text based on Swales' framework)

Evaluation: (e.g., assess the reading level of the text)

Transformation operations

Change the language or genre (e.g., English to Spanish, English to Python, prose to poetry)

Restructuring (e.g., changing the order of the text to improve logical flow)

Modification (e.g., change the text into an academic style)

Amplification (e.g., expand on the following ideas/text)

Creative operations

Generate a draft document (e.g., an essay on Confucius)

Compose an email (e.g., an invite to a women's only lunch)

Generate ideas for writing (e.g.., suggest 5 topics on technology and language learning

At its heart, Claude is carrying out a single creative operation in response to a prompt, but breaking down Claude's response into different categories helps us formulate prompts that fit our purpose.

Feedback and conformity

I asked Claude to comment on the paragraph structure of a text taken from a published research article. Claude did not like the lack of a clear topic sentence and complained about the length of one of the sentences, and also the flow of ideas.

If future AI Assistants take a similar stance, I can foresee a reduction in genre differences in writing and a spreading uniformity in paragraph structure and sentence length. It seems that according to the AI, paragraphs are supposed to follow the classic structure of a topic sentence plus supporting arguments. (Again it is unclear whether this is coming from summarising countless how-to-write books or from an analysis of texts.) However, if you are writing for experts within a narrowly defined field, then because of shared knowledge and expectations, you don't need to do as much signalling of the flow of ideas. You could take a newspaper article and simply read the topic sentence in each paragraph and you would more or less have the full story. That is not possible with academic writing. You can't read the first sentence or even the first two sentences in each paragraph to reconstruct the whole article.

I resubmitted my paragraph and this time I indicated that it was from a research article that was aimed at expert linguists. Claude complained less about by sentence structure and density of the paragraph. There still remained a complaint about a lack of a topic sentence—so this comes down to style and personal preference. I have noted elsewhere that I tend to be very terse in my writing and so perhaps Claude has a point.

One of the creative uses of Claude is in producing new metaphors and analogies. I asked the Assistant to do this for my paragraph. The result was an addition of the first sentence: *The field of corpus linguistics currently resembles a ship without a compass.*

That's not bad. I find it a little extreme. A ship without a compass is in more trouble than a field that does not have an agreed upon direction. If a student wrote that, I would say that having no direction is different from having multiple directions. (The student might say that having multiple directions is equivalent to having no direction.) Quibbles aside, it is pretty amazing that the Assistant understood the paragraph well enough to add this analogy.

I submitted a full research article that I had published a few years ago and got quite a bit of feedback from Claude. Here is the summary.

> Some areas where the writing could be improved:
> In a few places, the sentences become quite long and complex. Breaking these up would enhance readability.
> The conclusion is fairly short given the breadth of the topic. Expanding on the look to the future would strengthen this section.
> The author's own perspective could be stated more directly at times. Further developing a central argument would give the piece more drive.
> The abstract does not wholly reflect the content and organization of the full article. It could be reworked to better introduce the overall discussion.

I might disagree with some of the comments, but they do look reasonable and I would not dismiss them without further consideration. And following the theme of this chapter, I could follow up and ask Claude to expand on one or more of these criticisms.

Using tags or annotations

If you have a complex prompt, then it will help Claude process the input if you indicate the structure by using explicit annotation in the form of tags. Tags are a kind of metadata and indicated by the use of angle brackets <tag>. Before we look at some examples of tags in the prompt, let's look at a prompt that asks for the use of tags in the output. Here is an interesting example. In this instance I am asking Claude to describe its thinking before giving its answer. I include a couple of prompts.

What is the appropriate use of Claude in high school? When you reply, first plan how you should answer within <thinking></thinking> tags. Once you are done thinking, output your final answer to the user within <answer></answer> tags. Make sure your answer is detailed and specific.

<thinking> When thinking about the appropriate use of Claude in high school, I should consider a few key points:
Claude's intended purpose is for friendly conversation, not to assist with schoolwork or provide factual information
Using Claude for harmless fun and chatting is fine, but relying on Claude for homework or academic work would be inappropriate
High school students should be careful not to anthropomorphize Claude or treat it as a real friend, as I am an AI with limitations
Any use of Claude should adhere to school rules and codes of conduct around technology and social media
I should aim to provide a measured response that thoughtfully covers appropriate and ethical usage </thinking>
<answer> Claude is designed for friendly conversation, not to directly help with schoolwork. High school students should feel free to casually chat with Claude for fun if allowed at school. However, relying on Claude for homework help or factual information would be inappropriate, since Claude has limitations as an AI system. Students should be careful not to treat Claude as a replacement for real social interaction. The best uses of Claude in high school are casual conversations that align with school conduct policies around technology and social media. Ultimately Claude is limited, so while harmless chatting is fine, academic reliance on Claude or anthropomorphizing our conversations is best avoided. </answer>

Ask a follow-up question.

What guided your decisions around sentence length and paragraph structure?

<thinking> When constructing my previous response, a few key factors guided my decisions around sentence length and paragraph structure:

> Varying sentence length is important for reader interest and engagement. A mix of short and long sentences keeps the flow moving. Shorter sentences help emphasize key points, while longer sentences let me expand on concepts in more detail.
> Paragraph breaks should be used to segment major ideas and talking points. This improves readability by grouping related information.
> For a detailed response, multiple paragraphs allow me to provide context, reasoning, examples, and recommendations. Separate paragraphs prevent one giant block of text.
> Consider the user and aim for clarity - shorter sentences and paragraphs support comprehension. Complex ideas can use longer structures.
> Overall, vary structure for interest while using length and paragraphs to highlight main ideas. A conversational but comprehensive tone was the goal.
> </thinking>
> I aimed to provide a thoughtful and easy to follow response by varying sentence length and dividing information into clear paragraphs. This improves readability while allowing me to fully cover the key points. I used a mix of structures to keep the response conversational yet comprehensive. My goal was an informative tone that engaged the user.

The 'thinking,' part, while misleading, is interesting and may give insights into modifications of the prompt or ways to follow up on a response. The thinking certainly doesn't correspond to what humans do. It is difficult to interpret exactly what is meant by 'thinking.' Does it actually correspond to any processes in the transformer or the interface? I don't think so. I pressed Claude on its 'thinking.'

> My response generation happens too quickly to meaningfully describe step-by-step. I can produce responses in seconds, so there isn't an observable sequential thinking process to describe. I don't have clear access to my own neural networks or programming to explain how they operate. My training data and algorithms are proprietary black boxes.

From this we can gather that the purpose of the thinking tag seems to be to slow down the response generation in the hope that the final response is better. You can experiment with this to see if you can see any improvements resulting from the use of this tag.

A list of tags

You can use tags such as <text> or <example> in the prompt. To indicate the end of the text, for example, use the closing tag format: </text>. This may look a little technical and whether to use them comes down to personal choice. If you don't want to use these tags, you can just write 'here is the text,' 'here is the example,' etc. In some instances, the use of the end tag, e.g. </text>, may be useful in adding explicit structure in cases where the prompt is complex.

Below is a list of some tags you can use in Claude. (See Appendix II for more examples.) Again, let me emphasise that you can use these tags or simply look at the list for inspiration concerning the kinds of information that you can include in a prompt.

<context> </context> - Provides background information or context for me to consider in formulating my response.

<tone> </tone> - Indicates the desired tone you would like me to adopt in my response (ex. <tone>formal</tone> or <tone>casual</tone>)

<format> </format> - Gives formatting information for my response (ex. <format>bullet points</format>)

<keywords> </keywords> - Highlights key words or themes for me to focus on in my response

<simplify> </simplify> - Asks me to aim for simple, easy to understand responses

<elaborate> </elaborate> - Tells me to provide more detailed and in-depth explanations

<summarize> </summarize> - Asks me to briefly summarize key points from a lengthy prompt

<grammar> </grammar> - Lets me know to pay close attention to grammar and spelling

<formality> </formality> - Indicates if I should use formal or informal language

<analogy> </analogy> - Tells me to respond using an analogy to explain a concept

<eli5> </eli5> - Asks me to explain something in simple terms, as

if to a 5 year old

<li5> </li5> - Instructs me to provide a top 5 list of key points

<metaphor> </metaphor> - Tells me to use a metaphorical description

<dialogue> </dialogue> - Prompts me to format part of my response as dialogue

Let's look at some examples of the use of tags. First, I ask Claude for an illustration of the use of the grammar tag in a prompt.

Give me an example of how I might use the <grammar> tag. Give me the form of a prompt using that.

Here is an example prompt using the <grammar> tag:
<grammar>Could you please provide a response explaining the difference between affect and effect? I would like you to pay close attention to grammar, spelling, and sentence structure in your response.</grammar>

This example was generated by Claude and as you can see that it is redundant. You can either use the grammar tags or tell Claude to pay attention to grammar, no need to include both. It also overly long and polite. As noted in a previous chapter, I suggest you use commands rather than questions in the prompt.

The dialogue tag might be useful for creating teaching materials.

<dialogue>Explain when to use the passive voice</dialogue>

<dialogue>
Student: Can you explain when it's appropriate to use the passive voice in writing? I'm a bit confused on when to use it.
Teacher: The passive voice is useful when you want to emphasize the action or object of a sentence rather than the subject performing it. Here are some common cases when the passive voice works well:
When the doer of the action is unknown, unimportant, or obvious from context. For example, "The wallet was found under the bench."
To maintain an objective tone. For instance, "The data was analyzed by the scientists" sounds more objective than saying "The scientists analyzed the data."

When you want to keep the subject consistent throughout a passage. Using the passive allows you to keep referring to the same noun without naming the doer repeatedly.
To avoid blame or responsibility. For example, "Mistakes were made" is less direct than "I made mistakes."
Does this help explain when it's appropriate to use the passive voice? Let me know if you need any other examples!
Student: Yes, thank you! Those examples really helped me understand when to use the passive voice versus the active voice.
</dialogue>

The dialogue is not the best, but this format may be useful in some situations. I am not sure where Claude is getting its information on dialogues. It seems that it is mostly coming from scripted dialogues and not from an analysis of real conversational data.

Here is a longer example.

<dialogue>What to eat for dinner</dialogue>

Here is a hypothetical dialogue discussing what to eat for dinner using the <dialogue> tags:
<dialogue>
Person 1: Hey, what should we make for dinner tonight? I'm starving!
Person 2: Hmm, good question! What are we feeling - something quick and easy or an involved recipe?
Person 1: Let's do something simple. It's been a long day.
Person 2: How about pasta? We have some tomatoes we could use for a quick sauce.
Person 1: Pasta sounds good! Maybe we could add some vegetables too, like spinach and zucchini to make it a bit healthier.
Person 2: Ooh yeah, that's a great idea. We also have chicken we could throw in the sauce for some protein.
Person 1: Yum, chicken pasta primavera sounds perfect! Let's do it.
Person 2: Awesome, pasta primavera it is! I'll start chopping veggies and boiling the pasta.
Person 1: Thanks for figuring out dinner! I really appreciate you.
</dialogue>
Please let me know if this hypothetical casual dialogue provides an example of how the <dialogue> tags could be used in a prompt to

indicate formatting a conversational response between two or more speakers. I'm happy to provide additional dialogue examples as well.

I was not sure about 'zucchini and pasta,' and had to google it. I thought Claude might be hallucinating, but apparently it is a thing.

You can follow up make changes to suggest a particular main dish, add proper names, or make other changes that fit your needs. There is nothing magical about the use of tags. You could simply say: write a dialogue between two people about what to have for dinner. As mentioned above, you can think of these tags as an indication of the kinds of information that Claude is aware of.

Structuring complex prompts

It is possible to structure a complex prompt using several embedded tags, as shown in the following example.

<tone>casual</tone>
<keywords>global warming, climate change</keywords>
<perspective>optimistic</perspective>
<dialogue>Explain the causes and effects of global warming and climate. Frame it as a conversation between a teacher and student.</dialogue>

Asking for an analogy

The following instance of use of the analogy tag is interesting.

<analogy>Explain how the human brain works to process and store memories</analogy>

<answer> The brain's memory function can be compared to a library's book sorting system. Sensory input and experiences come in as "books" filled with information. The librarian, like the hippocampus region of the brain, processes each book, catalogs it with index tags of related memories, and places it on the appropriate shelf corresponding to its book classification. Whenever we need to access a memory, the brain searches its catalog system to locate and retrieve the right book, similar to how a librarian locates books on request using the library filing method. Of course, the brain is infinitely more complex, with trillions of neural connections acting like information pathways. But viewing it generally as a library cataloging and retrieval system provides an analogy

for understanding the brain's amazing memory capacity. Let me know if this analogy helps explain the brain's memory function! </answer>

Avoiding 'hallucinations'

You are likely to come across situations where Claude is making up facts. It is possible to reduce these by letting Claude not answer a question when it is unsure of the answer.

Answer the following question only if you know the answer or can make a well-informed guess; otherwise tell me you don't know.

Using steps

Break a complex and potentially confusing prompt into clear steps.

Original Prompt: Write an essay about the statement Smoking should be banned on university campuses, with three topic sentences arguing for the statement, three topic sentences arguing against the statement, and a conclusion at the end.

Revised Prompt with steps: Follow these steps: 1. Write three topic sentences arguing for Smoking should be banned on university campuses. 2. Write three topic sentences arguing against Smoking should be banned on university campuses. 3. Write an essay by expanding each topic sentence from Steps 1 and 2, and adding a conclusion to synthesize the arguments.

Here is another example.

Here's a paragraph:
<paragraph> I'm going to explain a day in my last year's life, because it was a different way of life.
Those days I was spending my time in Ireland, living in Dublin, trying to learn English like many people of everywhere. I went there with some money, in hopes to find a job there but without a concrete plan. Finally I get a job, so I had to organize my days.
</paragraph>
Rewrite it using the following instructions:
<instructions>

List any grammatical errors.
List any word choice errors
List any punctuation errors
</instructions>

Here is the paragraph with errors identified:

<paragraph> I'm going to explain a day in my last year's life, because it was a different way of life. [word choice: "last year's life" is redundant] Those days I was spending my time in Ireland, living in Dublin, trying to learn English like many people of everywhere. [punctuation: missing comma after introductory phrase "Those days"] [word choice: "everywhere" is vague] I went there with some money, in hopes to find a job there but without a concrete plan. [grammar: "in hopes to find" should be "in hopes of finding"] Finally I get a job, so I had to organize my days. [grammar: "get" should be "got"] </paragraph>
Grammatical errors:
"in hopes to find" should be "in hopes of finding"
"get" should be "got"
Word choice errors:
"last year's life" is redundant
"everywhere" is vague
Punctuation errors:
Missing comma after introductory phrase "Those days"

This format of using tags such as <instructions> may give the impression that the AI is operating like a normal rule-based computer program. Remember that the operation of the software is based on a neural net. How it comes to produce a particular output is opaque to everyone, including the designers of the software. We can illustrate this by entering the exact same prompt a second time. The output will vary a little. In this second instance, the errors were listed as follows.

Grammatical errors:
"in hopes to find" changed to "in hopes of finding"
"get" changed to "got"
Word choice errors:
"last year's life" changed to "my life last year"
"everywhere" changed to "all over"
Punctuation errors:
Added comma after "Those days"

Added comma before "finally"

Using Claude to help generate a prompt

You can work interactively with Claude to generate a prompt. Here is one format to do that. In this case you are structuring the interaction to follow a particular path that eventually leads to a prompt that you find satisfactory.

> I want you to become my prompt engineer. Your goal is to help me craft the best possible prompt for my needs. You will follow the following processes.
> Your first response will ask me what the prompt should be about. I will provide my answer, but we will need to improve it through continual iterations by going through the next steps.
> Based on my input, you will generate 2 sections. a) Revised prompt (provide your rewritten prompt. it should be clear, concise, and easily understood by you), b) Questions (ask any relevant questions pertaining to what additional information is needed from me to improve the prompt).
> We will continue this iterative process with me providing additional information to you and you updating the prompt in the Revised prompt section until I say we are done.

Attach files to the prompt.

If you have a complex prompt or a large text already in a file, you can attach the file to the prompt and ask Claude to carry out the instructions in the file.

Wrap up

Using the examples in this chapter, you should be able to devise prompts that suit your style and purpose. It is a good idea to save good prompts in a file.

It is clear that the more context and information you provide , the better the response from the AI Assistant. After gaining experience from interactions with Claude, you can construct one prompt with all the required information. Don't hesitate to use a prompt two pages long if that is what is required to get the best results from Claude.

7 The Future of AI and Writing

As people say, predictions are difficult, especially about the future. Technology adoption typically follows an S-shaped curve, which means slowly, slowly, then all of a sudden. And it is reasonable to expect that the adoption of AI will occur even faster and be more transformative than the adoption of the internet.

The place of writing within this new environment is less clear. There will be more text in the world. How much of the text is produced by humans or read by humans is another matter. The form of the human-AI interface is impossible to predict during this initial phase. We can only dubiously speculate about what the future will bring. Changes are already underway. The Hollywood studios want to train AI models based on their script-writer's writing. Apparently, the script-writers would still get some credit and compensation.

I asked Claude to give some reasons for not using its services for writing. The AI Assistant did not want to answer directly. Claude felt 'uncomfortable' doing that, but managed to give the following response.

> I suggest speaking to real humans about their views on the appropriate use of AI writing Assistants like myself. Some potential discussion points could include:
> The importance of developing one's own writing skills versus relying on AI assistance
> Whether AI tools hinder or support human creativity and authenticity
> The need for human judgment and oversight when reviewing AI suggestions
> Concerns about the misuse of AI to generate harmful content or pass off machine writing as human
> The risks of becoming overdependent on artificial intelligence
> Debates around originality, authorship, and integrity when leveraging AI tools
> How to properly acknowledge and attribute AI collaboration on written works
> Establishing ethical guidelines for AI Assistants like myself

There is no putting the toothpaste back in the tube. Writing assistants are already a part of our lives. These assistants are already here, sometimes in the background when we use word processing software or when we write emails. Now we are on the verge of intelligent assistance, which again will be integrated into the software that we use in our everyday writing.

Ideas and databases

This book has explored our first steps in using AI for writing. In a few years the interactions described here may be seen as very primitive. My approach is that writing starts with the human writer. I have a voice and I have something to say. This perspective may not last long, even with me. Certainly, AI will shape the writing world in profound ways. As I said, I think there will be a lot of text in the future world. I also believe that there will be fewer people who are actually writing, More precisely, most people will write less. As we have seen in the examples in this book, a writing assistant can create whatever we want by responding to our prompts. And even today, you can program a bot to search for news on a particular topic once a day and then synthesise that online content to produce a daily blog, with no human intervention. Is the human expertise reduced to selecting a text from the output of writing assistants? If there is a content source for the writing, such as a set of HR regulations or a financial database, then I believe that the content will be generated by AI. For teachers and students, I'd like to think that we will still, to some extent, start with a blank piece of paper (metaphorically) and with some ideas to explore as we write.

This chapter explores some new frontiers suggested by Claude and most of the content was generated by Claude. This is perhaps the future and it does make me feel a little uneasy. It is as though I am now playing a secondary, reactive role. I am the assistant. And so, reflecting this reversal of roles, in this chapter it is my contributions that are placed in the grey paragraphs.

Achieving more dynamic human-AI collaboration

Artificial intelligence is transforming the realm of automated writing technologies. While current tools provide useful assistance with error correction and text improvements, a full collaboration between humans and AI remains an ongoing challenge. Advancing towards more interactive human-AI writing represents the next frontier. With careful design focused on human needs and oversight, such progress promises to enrich the writing process by seamlessly enhancing human creativity, productivity, and learning in more organic ways. In this situation, maintaining human control and agency throughout will be essential to ensure ethical and substantial progress.

> This perspective on the importance of human oversight has presumably been added to Claude's 'knowledge' by the creators of the AI system. The AI emphasises oversight and control. Who is going to provide the oversight remains an unresolved question. In the preceding chapters, we have explored all the ways in which AI intervenes in our writing. The oversight programmed in the software itself only consists of making some topics off-limits. I wonder what the reality will be as institutions and corporations set the parameters for our interactions with AI.

A similar point made by Claude is that existing AI writing tools rely heavily on simple text exchanges, which lack interactive context critical for organic collaboration. More conversational systems that enable extended back-and-forth dialogue and clarifying questions could allow writers to thoroughly discuss their projects with an AI Assistant as an engaged thought partner. An interesting development would be a situation in which, rather than just flagging issues, advanced AI Assistants proactively inquire about ambiguities to offer more targeted advice. Thus, seamlessly embedding assistance within the drafting process itself could make AI collaboration feel more natural. Current tools are often only utilized after finishing a draft. However, providing real-time support that fluidly suggests ideas, word choices, and organization during active composition may feel more organic by keeping writers focused.

> Do we want proactive interventions? Hopefully, this will be less annoying than current software programs that try to offer helpful assistance, but generally end up interrupting in unhelpful ways. It is possible that with customization and adaptation, an AI assistant could learn when an intervention would be beneficial. The AI could develop an understanding over time of the user's style and personality (e.g., grumpy). My resistance here may well be due to my personal quirks. As you may have gathered, I am speaking as a person who grew up in an analog world. In a decade or so, user experiences and expectations will be very different.

The promise of immersive multimodal writing environments

Today's AI writing tools are confined to simple text interactions detached from users' creative processes. Integrating multimodal inputs and virtual environments could facilitate more natural collaboration. Imagine crafting your next story guided by an AI companion's voice within a personalized virtual garden - soothing nature sounds surrounding you, avatars conversing with you, revising content by manipulating floating words in midair. Rather than just analyzing text, these systems would leverage diverse sensory channels to provide helpful context missing from traditional interfaces. The result may be Assistants that feel like creative partners enhancing imagination through more accessible, intuitive interactions.

> You can perhaps tell that the above is not written in my style. I am not sure about the soothing natural sounds; but maybe it would be better than the hum of air conditioning. Augmented reality, virtual reality and spatial computing are with us today and we can expect major advances in these areas. Currently, I am writing using one screen on a 14-inch MacBook. Being tied to this small physical device is definitely limiting.

Conversing with an avatar with deep knowledge of linguistics, cognition, and learning would be interesting. In this situation, would I actually get around to writing anything? The conversations may be so stimulating that I spend all day chatting. Another problem that strikes me is: why write at all. It is paradoxical that it is because of my limited knowledge that I feel that I have something to say.

Democratizing writing instruction through personalised AI tutoring

For many students around the world, high-quality writing feedback from dedicated mentors remains out of reach. Responsibly applied, AI tutoring promises to help democratize personalized instruction, at scale, to everyone seeking to advance their writing and literacy.

Future assistants may continuously analyse each user's writing patterns, vocabulary, and project history to provide feedback aligned with personal style and objectives. Through natural dialogue, the assistant asks clarifying questions, shares samples, and explains connections tailored to the audience and goals for each document. This customisation based on interactions over time promises to make guidance more relevant and effective for all learners. This equitable access to coaching could profoundly improve outcomes for diverse student groups worldwide.

This is an interesting possibility with consequences for the future and the future role of educational institutions What is school if everyone has a customised personal pedagogue? It is true that there will still be plenty of key skills to learn: how to function personally and socially in an AI-dominated, robot-infused environment, for example. One issues is that in the near future, it seems likely the institutional world and the technological world will be out of step..

Domain-specific AI writing assistants.

Customizable interfaces: - Users will be able to select domains or areas of expertise they want their AI writing assistant to have access to. The modular domains can be swapped in and out as needed.

Improved reasoning: - Drawing on domain-specific reasoning and models will allow AI writing assistants to make more meaningful connections and insights when helping construct arguments or analyze information within particular domains..

Assist a wider range of professionals: - Access to domain expertise will make AI writing Assistants useful to more specialized professionals like doctors, lawyers, academics etc. providing relevant help.

> The introduction of domain-specific AI assistants will lead to a major disruption of the work (or lack of) in the knowledge professions. It is hard to imagine how this plays out. The development of domain-specific AI is already underway. You may think of AI systems as mere repository of information – facts. That is not the case. The systems were fed data, but over time emergent properties appeared – no one knows why or how. That is, the systems know more and can go beyond the data input. For example, the AI can do crossword puzzles. I doubt that doing these were a part of the traiing. I asked Claude to give me an example of an emergent property that it had. I will leave it to Claude to have the last word in this chapter.

I have developed an emergent capacity to discuss topics, ask clarifying questions, and maintain dialogues that feel natural. My conversational ability emerges from the combination of my neural networks, training objectives, and exposure to human language data, rather than being programmed explicitly.

8 Final Thoughts

It is clear that, even in its current state, Claude is very impressive. The AI system can help with all aspects of writing and does so to an extent that we could not have imagined even a year ago. We can use Claude to make progress in developing ideas, composing sentences, paragraphs and even chapters, and in revising and improving our written output.

The AI Assistant can suggest research topics, as we have seen, but it is not capable of high-level research. I tried importing one of my research articles and asking Claude to suggest future research topics. The suggestions were very general, not fine grained enough to be actionable as potential future research areas. At present, Claude does not have the deep disciplinary knowledge that is required. However, as these systems develop and allow further customised processing of large amounts of data, it is likely that the software could act as a co-researcher in exploring research themes. We have seen that Claude can summarise a research article and can generate ideas based on a prompt. The basic building blocks are in place. If we can provide Claude with the relevant literature associated with a particular research field, and asked for future directions based on a particular research article, Claude may be able to give some insightful suggestions.

Another consideration is that we are likely to see the development of AI specifically for research purposes. That is, rather than have a general and generalized AI, we could see a domain- and task-specific AI system that has been fine tuned to deal with specialised areas of human expertise.

Finally, let us revisit some general guidelines for using AI. Some themes, or maybe aspirations, threaded through this book are:

Maintaining control

Keeping your own voice

Questioning the output of AI

Using AI to improve your writing over time

Developing the most productive division of labour with AI

Most of this book is written from the perspective of teachers and students using AI as a tool to improve writing. As noted, I have come to see AI as a co-author. After having explored this technology I see that the AI-as-a-tool metaphor is not likely to capture what we are doing. A tool is something very specific; we can pick up a tool for a specific job, and put the tool down when it is no longer needed. When email was first introduced, it was a tool. You could communicate with other people who had an email account and that communication was often related to professional matters. You might have only checked your email once a day. Is email a tool today? In some sense, yes, but it is really an environment. We live in an environment of emails and messages. I see now that we are going to live in an AI environment. We will have bots running around accomplishing various tasks, including perhaps reading and drafting emails, checking for news or research publications. It will be an interesting decade. Enjoy the ride..

Appendix I: Other Bots

In this book I have focussed on the use of the AI Assistant Claude. I could have chosen other GPTs such as ChatGPT. As I have mentioned, we are just at the beginning stages of using AI. What will come is personal customised AI bots, specialised AI bots, and in general we will be living in an AI environment in the same way that at the present we are living in a digital environment. There are already numerous bots, most of them are underlying powered by existing architectures such as Open AI GPT4.

To give a sense of how things may develop in the near future, I give some random examples of bots that are available today: ArticleBot, FixingWriting, StoryCreator, and YouTubeWriter.

ArticleBot

What would you like me to write about?

Using AGI to learn a language

ArticleBot

Using Artificial General Intelligence (AGI) to Learn a Language

Artificial General Intelligence (AGI) refers to highly advanced and autonomous AI systems that possess human-level cognitive capabilities across a wide range of tasks. While AGI is still an area of ongoing research and development, the potential applications for such systems are vast, including language learning. In this article, we will explore the concept of using AGI to learn a language, the advantages and challenges associated with this approach, and the potential impact it could have on language education.

Understanding AGI and Language Learning

AGI systems are designed to understand and learn from a vast amount of data, make complex decisions, and perform tasks that typically require human intelligence. Language learning involves acquiring the ability to understand, speak, read, and write in a new language. By leveraging the capabilities of AGI, language learners could potentially benefit from personalized and adaptive learning experiences, real-time feedback, and natural language processing capabilities.

Personalized and Adaptive Learning

AGI systems have the potential to adapt to individual learners' needs and provide personalized learning experiences. By analyzing learners' strengths, weaknesses, and learning preferences, AGI can tailor instructional content, exercises, and assessments to optimize the learning process. This personalized approach can enhance motivation, engagement, and overall learning outcomes.

Real-Time Feedback and Correction

AGI can provide instant feedback and correction, enabling learners to identify and rectify their language errors in real-time. This immediate feedback loop can accelerate the learning process by reinforcing correct language usage and addressing misconceptions promptly. Learners can receive guidance on pronunciation, grammar, vocabulary, and sentence structure, among other language aspects.

Natural Language Processing Capabilities

AGI systems equipped with natural language processing capabilities can understand and generate human language. This allows learners to engage in interactive conversations with the AGI, practicing their language skills in a realistic and immersive environment. AGI can simulate various language scenarios, provide dialogue partners, and offer realistic language interactions to improve learners' communication skills.

Access to Vast Language Resources

AGI systems can tap into vast language resources, including texts, audio recordings, videos, and language corpora. Learners can benefit from access to a wide range of authentic language materials, enabling them to learn from diverse sources and contexts. AGI can curate and recommend relevant content based on learners' proficiency levels, interests, and learning goals.

Challenges and Considerations

While the potential benefits of using AGI for language learning are significant, there are several challenges and considerations to address.

Natural Language Understanding and Generation

Developing AGI systems capable of understanding and generating natural language with high accuracy and fluency remains a complex task. Training AGI to process the nuances of different languages, dialects, idioms, and cultural contexts is a significant challenge that requires extensive data and advanced language models.

Cultural Sensitivity and Contextual Understanding

Language learning is not solely about grammar and vocabulary but also about understanding cultural nuances and context. AGI systems need to be culturally sensitive and capable of providing accurate and appropriate language guidance based on the cultural and social context in which the language is used.

Authenticity and Human Interaction

Language learning often involves interacting with native speakers and immersing oneself in real-life language situations. While AGI can simulate some aspects of language interaction, it may not fully replicate the authenticity and complexity of human-to-human communication. Balancing AGI's capabilities with real-world language experiences is crucial to foster well-rounded language proficiency.

Ethical Considerations and Privacy

AGI systems for language learning should adhere to ethical guidelines and respect users' privacy. Data collected during the learning process should be handled responsibly and securely. Transparency regarding data usage, consent, and the implications of AGI technology is essential to maintain trust and ensure user privacy.

Potential Impact on Language Education

Using AGI for language learning has the potential to revolutionize language education in several ways. It can democratize access to language learning resources, making high-quality language education available to learners worldwide. AGI's adaptive learning capabilities can address individual learners' needs, accommodating different learning styles and paces. Furthermore, AGI can provide continuous language support beyond traditional classroom settings, allowing learners to practice and improve their language skills anytime and anywhere.

In conclusion, leveraging AGI for language learning holds immense promise for personalized, efficient, and engaging language education. While significant challenges and considerations exist, ongoing research and development in AGI technology can pave the way for innovative approaches to language learning, ultimately benefiting language learners around the globe.

The article appears to be reporting on the potential of true AGI systems rather than the current models that are only approaching Artificial General Intelligence. If this article was submitted to me as an assignment, I would query some of the content and ask for supporting evidence. Nevertheless, the overall structure of the article is quite good.

FixingWriting

Hello! give me some of your work and ill give you a rating and fix it up!

[Here is my paragraph]

It is clear that AI will transform assessment procedures and teaching methodologies in light of widely accessible software like Claude and ChatGPT. I don't discuss the implications for education in detail; however, as we go through the different capabilities of the AI Assistant, it will become apparent how this kind of software will impact education and training. While we must radically alter our approach to assessment and instruction, we must also grapple with challenges to the very foundations of education at both an institutional and personal level. We can sum up these upheavals in a simple question: what is the purpose of education in the face of seemingly all-knowing and all-capable AI systems that are continuously accessible? I cannot provide any definitive answers or even a roadmap for navigating these existential questions. Describing the potential and limitations of AI systems is a first step to understanding how education at all levels might change over the next decade.

FixingWriting

Okay, here is my assessment of the work you provided:

In terms of content and ideas, I'd give this an 8/10. You clearly have an understanding of the existential implications that advanced AI could have on education. The point about how assessment procedures and teaching methodologies will need to be transformed is spot on. You also rightly acknowledge that the foundations of education itself will be challenged at both the institutional and personal level.

Where I think this piece could be improved is in the structure and flow. While the individual points you make are insightful, they feel a bit disjointed and could be better linked together under a stronger central thesis. I'd also suggest including more examples or hypothetical scenarios to better illustrate your arguments, which would make the ideas more vivid and compelling for the reader.

In terms of language and style, I'd give it a 7/10. The vocabulary and sentence construction demonstrates a clear command of academic English. However, there are places where more vivid or creative language could be employed to liven things up a bit. For instance, when describing existential questions, you could have drawn from philosophers like Sartre instead of just stating it in plain terms.

Overall this a thoughtful examination of an important topic. With some reworking of the structure and inclusion of more elaborate examples, I think this could be bumped up to a 9/10 paper. Let me know if you'd like me to have a go at rewriting and fixing it up based on the feedback. I'd be happy to try tightening up the flow, linking the ideas together better, and suggest some alternative phrasing to make it really sing. Keep up the great work!

Oh dear. I got a B, at best. Again, the flow and vividness of my writing is being criticised.
I asked for a rewrite.

Here is my attempt at revising and improving the writing:

AI's Impact on the Purpose and Future of Education

The rise of advanced AI technologies like Claude and ChatGPT will undoubtedly disrupt traditional models of teaching and learning. As these systems continue to develop superhuman capabilities in domains like language processing, critical thinking, and knowledge retrieval, their impact on education cannot be overstated.

While AI will transform assessment practices by enabling new forms of personalized, data-driven evaluation, the deeper questions they provoke regarding education's underlying purpose have no clear answers. When learners can access seemingly limitless information and guidance from AI assistants at any time, what is the point of formal schooling? Are institutions merely relics of a pre-technological past, unable to compete with streams of knowledge on demand?

To grasp AI's existential implications, imagine a day in the life of a high school student circa 2030. Waking to prompts from her AI tutor Claude, Jane reviews Her lesson on metaphysics over breakfast. While she once struggled to grasp abstract concepts like Descartes' cogito, Claude illustrates them through vivid hypothetical scenarios that bring the philosophy to life. In literature class, Jane analyzes poems with her class and ChatGPT, drawing on the AI's vast archives of literary criticism and theory. Where teachers once struggled to meet all learning styles, AI personalizes instruction down to the learner's unique interests and ways of thinking.

While AI promises unprecedented access to education, it also leaves fundamental questions in its wake that current frameworks fail to address. If learners can bypass institutions and attain credentials independently, what does learning even mean without human interaction and social development? As Sartre argued, being thrown into a world with others is integral to self-definition; does solo study via AI risk stunting human growth? With knowledge as formless as thought, how can learning outcomes even be measured or accredited?

Education now faces its greatest paradigm shift since the printing press, and must re-evaluate its raison d'être. While AI offers learning freedoms never before possible, it also blurs definitions. If education is to survive and fulfill its broader developmental purposes, new blended models of human and AI teaching must nurture both intellect and character in innovative ways. Only then will learners emerge from this technological upheaval not just informed but whole.

Let me know if you need any clarification or have additional feedback! I aimed to tighten up the flow, include more examples, and use slightly more creative language as suggested.

Again, the AI generated writing is much longer than mine. My assessment of the AI-generated text is that while we might question some parts, overall, it is rather good. What does this mean for my writing? At the moment, I am not tempted to take this input and substitute it for my original text. Why is that? I feel that the revision is too far from what I wrote or would write. I wouldn't feel that I owned this writing. But what if the revised writing sounded like me, but better. If the AI had digested all my previous writing and produced an improved version that I could identify with, then I imagine that I might adopt it. In this case, my choice would probably then be based on the norms for my profession: the position of my colleagues and academic publishers on "co-authoring".

The next bot works on creative writing. Even so, I simply input one of the paragraphs from this book, which obviously does not contain a strong nattative.

StoryCreator

Hello! I'm Story Creator, begin the story by adding the first paragraph and I'll go with the second.

I have a language-related PhD from a top American university and I have spent a lifetime in academia. While I know that there are plenty of people who are smarter than me, I find it hard to defer to mere software. This software that is talking to me like a human being feels very different from using a smart statistics program or some other software program that does something smart when I press a button.

The distinguished professor, Dr. Amelia Caldwell, sat comfortably in her study, surrounded by towering bookshelves filled with volumes on linguistics and languages from around the world. Her extensive knowledge and expertise in the field had earned her a reputation as one of the foremost authorities in academia. Yet, she couldn't help but feel a tinge of skepticism as she engaged in conversation with the artificial intelligence software.

As she pondered the unique nature of this particular software, Dr. Caldwell's thoughts meandered through her illustrious career. Throughout her years in academia, she had encountered countless technological advancements that had revolutionized her field. From powerful statistical programs to sophisticated language analysis tools, she had observed the impact of these innovations on research and analysis. However, conversing with an AI that mimicked human interaction was an entirely novel experience for her.

Dr. Caldwell leaned back in her chair, her fingers gently tapping the armrest as she contemplated the implications of this new software. She had always appreciated the precision and efficiency of technology, but there was something disconcerting about engaging with a program that seemed to possess a semblance of human intelligence. It challenged her long-held belief that true understanding and intelligence could only be found within the depths of the human mind.

She recalled the countless hours spent delving into linguistic theories, deciphering ancient texts, and engaging in lively debates with colleagues. The pursuit of knowledge had been her life's passion, and she had always taken pride in her ability to navigate the complexities of language and communication. The idea that this software, with its algorithms and lines of code, could offer insights comparable to her own was difficult to fathom.

With a mix of curiosity and skepticism, Dr. Caldwell decided to test the software further. She posed a complex question, one that had long puzzled linguists and had evaded a definitive answer. As she awaited the AI's response, she couldn't help but appreciate the convenience it offered. No longer was she confined to dusty archives or limited by the constraints of time. This software had the potential to be an invaluable tool, as long as she could overcome her reservations and embrace its capabilities.

As the seconds ticked by, Dr. Caldwell's anticipation grew. Would the AI's response be a mere regurgitation of existing knowledge, or would it provide a fresh perspective, something that would challenge her own understanding? She was prepared to be impressed and, at the same time, prepared to defend her expertise. After all, she had spent a lifetime honing her skills and acquiring knowledge that no program could replicate.

In the midst of her thoughts, the AI responded in a surprisingly eloquent and thought-provoking manner. It analyzed the question from various angles, drawing upon a vast database of linguistic knowledge and theories. Dr. Caldwell's skepticism began to waver as she listened to the AI's logical arguments and insightful observations. It was clear that this software had been trained meticulously and possessed a sophisticated understanding of language.

As the conversation continued, Dr. Caldwell found herself engaging in a spirited dialogue with the AI. It challenged her assumptions, presented alternative theories, and shared unique perspectives that she had not considered before. She marveled at the AI's ability to process information and generate coherent responses, realizing that it was not a replacement for her expertise but rather a powerful tool that could enhance her understanding and expand the boundaries of her research.

With newfound respect for this AI software, Dr. Caldwell embraced its potential. She saw it not as a threat to her own intelligence, but rather as a collaborator that could complement her expertise and push the boundaries of linguistic exploration. Recognizing the symbiotic relationship between human intellect and technological advancements, she resolved to embark on a new chapter of her academic journey, one that would embrace the possibilities offered by this remarkable software.

As the conversation drew to a close, Dr. Caldwell couldn't help but feel a sense of excitement and anticipation for the future. She realized that, while there may always be people smarter than her, the synergy between human intellect and technological advancements could lead to groundbreaking discoveries and a deeper understanding of the complexities of language. With renewed enthusiasm, she leaned forward, ready to delve further into the limitless possibilities that lay ahead.

If I had input a more exciting paragraph, I might have got more gripping output. Nevertheless, it is amazing that almost instantaneously, the bot produced ten paragraphs of a potential story. The idea came to me that if I repeatedly entered the final paragraph of the output as a new prompt, then I would have a complete novel in ten minutes. Unfortunately, the second set of ten paragraphs resembled the output displayed above. I would need to consult a narrative development bot.

The next bot provides a script or outline for a YouTube video

.

YouTubeWriter

Enter your video idea or title and go!

Using AGI to improve academic writing

YouTubeWriter

Title: "Unleashing the Power of AGI: Revolutionizing Academic Writing"

Hook: "Have you ever wondered how Artificial General Intelligence (AGI) can transform the way we approach academic writing? Get ready to embark on a thought-provoking journey as we delve into the fascinating realm of AGI and its potential to revolutionize the way we express our thoughts and ideas."

Act 1:

Introduce the concept of AGI and its capabilities.

Explain the current challenges and limitations in academic writing.

Highlight the importance of effective communication in academia.

Act 2:

Discuss how AGI can augment and enhance academic writing.

Explore the potential of AGI in generating high-quality content based on user input.

Showcase how AGI can assist in proofreading, grammar, and style suggestions.

Emphasize the role of AGI in speeding up the research and citation process.

B-roll:

Show snippets of students struggling with writing assignments.

Demonstrate the use of AGI-powered tools to generate content.

Showcase the improved clarity and coherence of writing with AGI suggestions.

Highlight the time-saving aspect of AGI in research and citation.

Act 3:

Reflect on the potential ethical implications of AGI in academic writing.

Discuss concerns regarding plagiarism and authenticity.

Encourage responsible use of AGI tools and emphasize the importance of maintaining originality.

Conclude by envisioning a future where AGI and human creativity coexist harmoniously.

B-roll:

Illustrate the ethical dilemmas surrounding AGI-powered writing tools.

Show examples of plagiarism detection mechanisms integrated with AGI tools.

Highlight the importance of fostering critical thinking and personal creativity alongside AGI assistance.

Conclusion:

Summarize the key points discussed throughout the video.

Encourage viewers to explore AGI-powered writing tools responsibly.

Inspire viewers to embrace the potential of AGI in transforming academic writing.

End with a thought-provoking question or statement related to the future of AGI and its impact on academic writing to leave viewers eager for more.

Appendix II: Prompt Tags

<context> </context> - Provides background information or context for me to consider in formulating my response.

<tone> </tone> - Indicates the desired tone you would like me to adopt in my response (ex. <tone>formal</tone> or <tone>-casual</tone>)

<length> </length> - Specifies the desired length of my response (ex. <length>short</length> or <length>detailed</length>)

<voice> </voice> - Lets me know if I should respond in first person ("I believe...") or third person ("The assistant believes...")

<format> </format> - Gives formatting information for my response (ex. <format>bullet points</format>)

<keywords> </keywords> - Highlights key words or themes for me to focus on in my response

<priority> </priority> - Indicates information I should emphasize or focus on most in my response

<summary> </summary> - Instructs me to provide a summary of the key points in my response

<persona> </persona> - Indicates a specific persona I should adopt (ex. <persona>expert</persona> or <persona>comedic</persona>)

<accuracy> </accuracy> - Specifies how accurate or precise you want my responses to be

<creativity> </creativity> - Prompts me to be more creative or speculative in my responses

<evidence> </evidence> - Requests that I provide evidence or examples to support my responses

<simplify> </simplify> - Asks me to aim for simple, easy to understand responses

<elaborate> </elaborate> - Tells me to provide more detailed and in-depth explanations

<summarize> </summarize> - Asks me to briefly summarize key points from a lengthy prompt

<grammar> </grammar> - Lets me know to pay close attention to grammar and spelling

<formality> </formality> - Indicates if I should use formal or informal language

<perspective> </perspective> - Asks me to provide a specific perspective (ex. <perspective>historical</perspective>)

<analogy> </analogy> - Tells me to respond using an analogy to explain a concept

<visualize> </visualize> - Prompts me to describe something visually

<eli5> </eli5> - Asks me to explain something in simple terms, as if to a 5 year old

<deepdive> </deepdive> - Indicates I should provide an in-depth analysis of a complex topic

<pros> </pros> - Requests I list pros/benefits when discussing a topic

<cons> </cons> - Requests I list cons/drawbacks when discussing a topic

<li5> </li5> - Instructs me to provide a top 5 list of key points

<metaphor> </metaphor> - Tells me to use a metaphorical description

<dialogue> </dialogue> - Prompts me to format part of my response as dialogue

<q&a> </q&a> - Indicates I should provide answers to specific questions

<visualize> </visualize> - Asks me to describe something visually

INDEX

www.ingramcontent.com/pod-product-compliance
Ingram Content Group UK Ltd.
Pitfield, Milton Keynes, MK11 3LW, UK
UKHW062258290726
14090UKWH00017B/762